Return from Exile

Return from Exile

Revelations from an Anchoress in St. Augustine

Maury,
a friend of a
friend

MARIE LAURE

Marie Laure

RESOURCE *Publications* · Eugene, Oregon

RETURN FROM EXILE
Revelations from an Anchoress in St. Augustine

Resource Publications
An Imprint of Wipf and Stock Publishers
199 W. 8th Ave., Suite 3
Eugene, OR 97401

www.wipfandstock.com

PAPERBACK ISBN: 978-1-6667-0763-2
HARDCOVER ISBN: 978-1-6667-0764-9
EBOOK ISBN: 978-1-6667-0765-6

08/06/21

"Peregrinate." Book Cover with permission from artist Leah Palmer Preiss.

For my mother and my daughter

"*And from the time that this was shown, I often longed to know what our Lord meant. And fifteen years and more later my spiritual understanding received an answer, which was this: 'Do you want to know what your Lord meant? Know well that love was what he meant. Who showed you this? Love. What did he show? Love. Why did he show it to you? For love.*"

JULIAN OF NORWICH, REVELATIONS OF DIVINE LOVE

Contents

Contents

Preface

"I love you to that supermoon and back," we wrote to each other.

At predawn, the supermoon drops down toward the horizon through crepe-myrtle leaves on a tree within reach of my desk. I hear two "early birds" call to each other, sending their own private messages.

"To the moon and back" is the familiar call my daughter and I share from anywhere in the world. I look at the moon photos we exchanged via email last evening; hers, from Rock Harbor on Cape Cod; mine, from the San Sebastian River in St. Augustine, Florida.

Hannah, soon to reach her thirtieth year, lives in the place we once called home. Sometime after graduating from college, she boomeranged, but I had already moved south to a second home in Florida.

When I was thirty, I found myself alone in the world. The man for whom I had fallen head-over-heels had come and gone. Time stopped there. My life was never the same. He changed me. It marked a before and after moment in my life.

As the dawn breaks, the moon disappears into pink clouds beyond a tall palm tree. It will return tonight over the river on the other side of the house. I'll be waiting for it on my river porch.

For women, waiting is like a familiar face one no longer notices. We wait nine months for our babies. Then we wait for them to grow up. Then we wait for them to call.

Learning to wait is not a bad thing. It comes in handy at times when the world does not cooperate with our plans. These days, the entire world is waiting for a pandemic to pass. Much of our day-to-day living has been suspended indefinitely. We want to see our family and friends, but we don't want to get sick or die.

At the age of thirty, a woman named Julian fell ill in Norwich, England, during the Black Death Plague in the fourteenth century. Her mother waited at her bedside for days. Julian's fever would not break. Her mother watched through the nights and days, waiting to close her daughter's eyes. Finally, she called for a priest. Her daughter was dying. Something unthinkable for any mother in any century. I was not there, but I am sure they were crying, hugging, and praying harder than ever before.

In the midst of the current coronavirus crisis, I not only can imagine how desperately Julian's mother would have wanted her daughter to pull through, but I also understand how much fear, anxiety, worry, and death must have filled their thoughts, their home, their village. Our twenty-first-century pandemic has allowed me to identify with them in ways that before were impossible.

In the end, Julian survived. During her near-death episode, she saw her "Beloved," her "one and only." This forever changed her and the trajectory of her life. I have never had such a near-death experience, but losing love felt like that for me. At age thirty, like my daughter, like Julian, life stretched out over a far-away horizon that I could not see beyond, no matter how I tried. The horizon is still out there, but my vantage point has changed. I no longer try to see what lies ahead.

The bright morning sun is beginning to cast itself like diamonds across the river beyond my "lanai," the word Floridians have borrowed from Hawaiians to describe a small screened-in room. I call this little lanai my "anchorage." Julian lived out her last years in such a room. Hers was an actual anchorage, a very small room attached to a church, where as an "anchoress," she was locked in for good—for the rest of her life. The word "anchorage" comes from the Greek word, anachoreo, which means to withdraw.

As she tells in her story, *A Revelation of Love*, Julian saw Jesus when she lay dying. She could never forget those visions of him. He would be forever her "one and only" love. She later wrote about this experience so she could understand why this happened to her at age thirty. She threw over everything else for him to become an anchoress at age fifty.

Julian and I never met, of course, but I feel like we have. Last summer I sat alone in her anchorage in Norwich. I traveled there because I wanted to sit "with her" there. I wanted to understand why she decided to attach herself to a church from the age of fifty until her death, which came some decades later, according to informed estimates. This woman's story of exile had been calling me from across the ocean. I, too, have been living in self-imposed exile.

The choice for such an exile is an interesting one. Other women in the Middle Ages, given their limited options, also chose the life of an anchoress over getting married or living in a convent. It was not for everyone, that's for sure. I would never have considered it when I was thirty. I could not even have imagined it. We do not think as much about dying as we do about living at that age. That's natural. Why would anyone choose to go into exile? For me, finding the answer, has felt like being pulled through the eye of a needle, or a narrow gate. Once through it, nothing is ever the same.

Acknowledgments

This book was midwifed into being with the help of my beloved River Writers: Ann, Michael, Roger, and most especially, Cheryl and her teacher's red pen. I thank each of you from my heart of hearts for your genuine care and support. I couldn't have done it without y'all.

To my husband and copy editor, Lance Carden, for always giving generously of your time and attention to my pursuit of words. It is impossible to say how grateful I feel as this work, at long last, comes to fruition. Muchas gracias por todos.

PART ONE

Exiled

A Tree Cannot Know Exile

Spring 2018

A small writers group has been gathering on my river porch on the San Sebastian River for more than two years. One of them is a native Floridana-Menorcan woman who embodies living history in this ancient city of St. Augustine.

"You are my cloister," she said softly but emphatically one evening, looking at each of our faces.

Nobody needed an explanation. Her word "cloister" fit perfectly with my own sense of sanctuary in my home, which for me has been a place of exile. In the early years when I visited here, often alone, I loved to lock the door behind me and stay put. The birds flying by or diving into the water, or the dolphins occasionally swimming silently by in the river, were all that I needed of the outside world. I never thought of this home as anything but a refuge in those days—those days being before my daughter's father bailed out, or as our marriage counselor aptly put it: "He hung a left." Indeed, he did.

Before the "bailout," each visit to the Florida townhouse was a respite from hectic home and office work. It was my escape. At first, it didn't go much further than that in my mind, needing little explanation or excuse. It was a simple three-hour flight, and it offered a place with few, if any, memories. As yet. Absent the stories of a place, the place itself is simply that. One just enters in and finds peace. Cloisters are like that.

I've known such an empty-space feeling while on retreat in the cloisters of convents and monasteries. They hold others' stories, but not my own. I knew peace and silence awaited me there. So, for a time, I thought of this St. Augustine residence as a refuge releasing me from my worldly self. Nobody but me and that "Afrika tree" standing guard over the river could know the secrets within, the secrets in my heart. That tree has been and continues to be the one and only constant here. I have written poetry about it—love poems. It's been a twenty-year affair. Could I ever leave it? Do I wish to? What in it speaks to me?

The speaking once was one-way, only me to it, but all that has changed now that I live every day in communion with it. One day, when my three young grandchildren shared lunch on the lanai, I said: "That tree has seen everything that has happened on this lanai." It sparked a spontaneous trip down memory lane for me and them. During the early days here, my life was topsy-turvy. I shared my sad feelings with my tree friend while sitting alone in the screened enclosure. There was never a time when I was in need that the tree was not there and available. For me, that tree is sacred. It represents the "one and only."

For years, as I was coming and going from this place of refuge (before I was exiled here), I took it for granted that the tree would always be standing there. It always is. Neither hurricanes nor violent thunderstorms have snapped it from its rooted spot. After two decades, I know we are connected, in part because we are here together in this place at the same time.

A tree might seem to be just a tree, but Longfellow and others have shared with the world their love for their own leafy friends. These living, breathing, sacred ones make a place what it is. They can be a place of belonging for anyone who sits at their feet to ponder or to read, or just lean one's back against some rough bark, feeling welcome to stay as long as one likes. One is at home there. A tree is deeply rooted in place, never to wander from where it began. A tree cannot know exile. But it may know more about a place—one's place in the world—than we do.

For some of us, the notion of living and dying in the same place speaks of no life at all. I felt that way when I was young and

wandering through my own proverbial forty years in the d(
Truth be told, I could not understand anyone wanting to stay put
for any period of time. I did not go far, for all my moving about.
But for me it was better than standing still. Choosing the Florida
townhouse during a divorce in my fifties, gave me an opportunity to
move someplace new. I arrived just in time to begin my "third life."
For me, no longer raising children, no longer a full-time worker,
no longer an active grandmother, a certain freedom has come in
the form of exile. How is it that standing in one place, like my tree
friend, feels like a relief? Maybe the answer is found in a little encounter between a woman and a third-century monk.

Abba Serapion was one of the "Desert Fathers." These were
hermits, monks and ascetics who lived in the desert in Egypt in
the very early days of Christianity. He was known as an incessant
wanderer. One day, he learned about a female recluse. Skeptical of
her way of life, he traveled a great distance to meet her. As the story
goes, he asked her:

"Why are you sitting here?"

"I am not sitting; I am on a journey,"[1] she replied.

---

1. Ward, "The Desert of the Heart." wordpress.com

There's No Place Like Home

July 21, 2018

Two weeks from tonight I will be in the air between Boston and London, that "liminal space" above the Atlantic. It won't be the first time I travel across the ocean by myself, perhaps not the last. Why go? Home is fine, lovely in fact. I love the summer sounds of cicadas hissing and frogs croaking. But most of the birds are now free to come and go; their nesting season is complete.

"It's good to know you can still do things alone," I had said earlier today to a young hairdresser and to myself in the mirror. "The day I return will be my sixth-fifth birthday." It screams for a marker—and not just marking time.

Buddhists speak of the "auspicious time" to do something. Some years ago, I was invited to a Buddhist wedding. When the clock struck the appointed hour, neither bride nor groom appeared. One of the monks explained to those of us uninitiated in Buddhism that we were simply to wait for them as they would know when it was the "auspicious time" to marry. At least forty-five minutes, filled with chatter and chanters, passed before they showed up . . . together.

I never forgot that idea of an "auspicious" time, because it felt so unlike the rigid scheduling we in the West expect. Travel often challenges those expectations. Time always seems a little different when one is away from home, particularly in a foreign country. For communication purposes, I would have to get used to the fact that

Great Britain is five hours ahead of Florida. When I am awakening over there, my husband, Arthur, will be sleeping. To communicate, we'll have to wait for the auspicious time to present itself.

One day, when Arthur and I were in Italy, as I sat at the computer, I saw something pop up on the lower edge of the screen, saying: *Hannah is online.* Without a second thought, I clicked my cursor on it. Suddenly, my daughter was on the screen, working at her potter's wheel in a college studio.

"Hi Mom!" she said, smiling up at me from around the world. I can still picture her, bent over, elbow deep in clay, hair pulled up on top of her head. The auspicious time had brought us face to face.

I have decided this is the auspicious time for a pilgrimage because it is calling me. It all starts with that call, as I learned fifteen years ago, when I wrote a graduate thesis about pilgrimage. I chose that subject, even though I had never actually been a pilgrim. I had, however, been on other journeys, which I had called pilgrimages.

For instance, there was a road trip with my daughter to some of the National Parks during their centennial year in 2016. That certainly evoked the pilgrim spirit, as did a solo trek to Hopi land, in Arizona, to learn about the most reclusive of indigenous peoples, the Hopi, "people of peace." Yet for neither trip, nor for any other, had I ever prepared for a pilgrimage as pilgrims are supposed to do. This time is different.

The seed was planted years ago. It began germinating and sprouting in early 2018. All the signs seemed to point to it, even before I knew where or when to go. The "call" came first. When I heard it from deep down, I wrote this: "It's time—the fullness of time—God's time." It was the auspicious time.

My preparations began several months ago. After much consideration, I decided to go to England to see where the anchoress Julian of Norwich lived, wrote, and prayed. The Black Death of her time had spared few. Julian herself saw the face of death. She wrote about experiencing sixteen so-called visions, or "showings," which she believed saved her life. She then felt compelled to write about them during years of self-imposed exile that ended in death.

Julian has lain quiet and still for over six hundred years, perhaps contemplatively awaiting the auspicious moment when the world's needs would call for her again. Although I could not yet know it, my pilgrimage to Norwich would bring the past and the present together during another pandemic, another dark time in the world.

What might life have been like for Julian during the plague? From the age of six through thirty, she and her family, her village, her community-at-large lived in the shadow of the "Great Pestilence" or "Great Mortality," otherwise called the "Black Death."

As a result, Norwich, once a vibrant port in the easternmost county of England, lost most of its trade and commerce with northern Europe. The village markets closed. The churches, a center of life for many, locked their doors. Death was in the air every day and night. Julian and her mother would have known many losses. Priests brought the "last rites" from house to house. Relief was nowhere in sight. Everyone suffered, both economically and otherwise. Those who survived faced an entirely different life: Familiar faces were gone, shops were shuttered. There were scarcities of supplies and other daily necessities. For many, there was a loss of hope.

When Julian was twenty, in 1362, the second wave of the plague swept through Norwich. Once again, the Black Death took its toll without discriminating between the old, the young, the rich, the poor, the male, the female, the elitist, the tradesman, the Christian, or the Jew.

Ten years later, in 1373, it was Julian's turn. At age thirty-and-a-half, living with her mother, she fell extremely sick with a fever that would not break. The priest came with his crucifix. He held it at the foot of Julian's deathbed. Through fever-pitched eyes, she began to envision the Passion of Jesus Christ on the Cross. For three days, Julian felt his suffering, saw his bleeding, knew his pain.

"And in all this time of Christ's pain the only pain I felt was for the pain of Christ,"[1] said Julian.

Suddenly, her fever broke. Julian did not die, but her near-death experience changed her life. She would never forget those visions, or "showings," even as she returned to village life.

1 Spearing, *Revelations of Divine Love,* 67.

Twenty years later, that unforgettable experience ultimately led her to become an anchoress, committing herself to live the rest of her life in a cell, where she would write *A Revelation of Love*. It is a book of hope based on her unfolding understanding of being at one with the Divine. She wrote about hope during a plague that many viewed as a punishment from God for their sins.

She had no way of knowing at the time that eventually she would become the first woman to have a book published in English.

Resistance

July 2018

In the week leading up to my well-planned, long-thought-out pilgrimage, resistance reared its ugly head in the form of questions:

"Why go? Why now?" I asked myself.

I tried unsuccessfully to coax my husband to join me at the last minute on what was designed to be a solo pilgrimage. Where was the resistance coming from? Some in my circle said it was the "evil one" at work. Not one to use that terminology, or to think in terms of opposing forces "out there," I rejected this out of hand. Yet, I could not deny that a sense of uncertainty was creeping in. This resistance was not to the place, Julian of Norwich's anchorage in England, but to something less obvious: I was sure the pilgrimage would bring change. It must.

To bring back the "boon" of the pilgrimage, one must give up something for the sacred. Pilgrimage calls for sacrifice.

"Kairos" that "god of serendipity," if allowed would see to it that something happens on the pilgrimage that is lasting and meaningful, and thereby a game changer. Taking the first step in that direction is the way forward, but also perhaps the moment of no turning back. Buried within the resistance to change was my total understanding that no one else could fulfill this particular call. What, I wondered, would it mean to follow through? There is no way to know from the safety and comfort of home. Surrendering to the unknown possibilities takes trust and faith that *"All shall be well,"*[1] in Julian's oft-quoted words.

"Pilgrimage starts the wheel . . . it turns the wheel of life, and we have to live with the consequences,"[2] writes Phil Cousineau in "The Way of Serendipity," a chapter in *The Art of Pilgrimage.*

---

1. Spearing, *Revelations of Divine Love*, 24.
2. Cousineau, *The Art of Pilgrimage*, 119.

No Go!

August 3, 2018

"We are not loading any more passengers," said the flight attendant with her hand up in front of my face. My boarding pass had just been scanned. I was next to board.

"What's going on?" I asked.

"Tornadoes in Boston have closed Logan Airport to incoming flights," she answered.

"Tornadoes in Boston? What? When has there ever been a tornado in Boston?" I wondered, having lived in Massachusetts most of my life.

The entire shutting down of my only option to cross the Atlantic Ocean appeared to me like a giant red STOP sign.

As I gathered myself and my luggage, I stared outside at the white puffy clouds floating by in the bright-blue Florida sky. It seemed to be a perfect day to fly. I was now waiting for an announcement regarding departure to Boston. My evening flight to England was still scheduled to go out of Boston's Logan Airport, despite its closure to my incoming flight. I sensed something spiritual in this unexpected "watching and waiting." I sat as if in my own world, trying to tune out all the voices of disgruntled would-be passengers.

"It is not the auspicious time to go. I am not going to England," I said under my breath. I already knew it. During the wait, I remembered that I had uncharacteristically taken out travel insurance in case of some unforeseeable interruption. I was certain the option to go had already been foreclosed. I simply sat for the next three-plus hours, waiting for the final decision by the airline to come. And it did: No go! I was officially grounded.

Back at home later that day, I pondered this unexpected turn of events. The "Why go?" of previous days had become "Why not?" I had set my intention when I first had a sense of "call" to make a pilgrimage. Most especially, this was to be a quest to understand the meaning behind self-imposed exile. Dame Julian had been called to it, and I felt more and more a sense of exile in my own life. Her exile and my sense of exile had moved me through six months of preparations. I was to visit Norwich to learn something of Julian's life by walking where she would have walked in the fourteenth century. Her anchorage was calling me, as perhaps it had called her over six centuries ago.

Sometime during the planning phase, I began to consider the pilgrimage in wider terms. Why not include Canterbury? After all, Chaucer, one of Julian's contemporaries, had told tales of pilgrimages, in what became the classic pilgrimage book, *The Canterbury Tales* published in 1476, two centuries before Julian's book in 1670. What did one have to do with the other? Nothing.

Without realizing it, I had usurped my own pilgrimage plans, shortchanging Julian for Chaucer. I was also muddying the original intent of my pilgrimage. Tiny St. Julian's Church was being overshadowed by gigantic Canterbury Cathedral. It could not be justified as part of my pilgrimage. However, that did not stop me from making all the arrangements to go to Canterbury, in addition to Norwich.

When the "way" did not open at the airport, I sensed immediately the reason had something to do with my bending the original intention to my will rather than simply honoring the call. I knew I had to let the whole thing go.

Perhaps I was not truly prepared to meet the mystical Julian. The auspicious time was not this time. I knew deeply that this was the truth. Divine intervention spoke clearly to me that morning in the airport: "No. Not now." I had been spared the "desolation of success." In other words, when we do not find what we are seeking to find; receive what we ask to receive; get what we think we want, the mystery is not diminished. There will be another time, God's time.

That I did not have to leave Florida to learn something is the truth behind my aborted pilgrimage. The critical moment for crossing the proverbial threshold had not arrived.

A wave of relief came over me. I saw clearly that I did not have to travel to find what I already knew: I am a woman in the midst of exile in her own backyard, like the woman who said to the monk Serapion: *"I am not sitting; I am on a journey."*[1]

I know that I am on a journey, somewhere between being an anchoress or becoming an itinerant monk who wants to walk away from everything. Hindus have a name for someone who wanders away at this phase of life: A "forest dweller." To become a forest dweller, one simply leaves; the pilgrim, on the other hand, takes a step out from the normal world, but only a step; an anchoress remains in the anchorage.

Pilgrimage, by definition, has a point of departure and a point of return. It is qualified as such. Without the return, the pilgrimage is incomplete. The forest dweller has no destination and no intention to return. Sometimes I wonder how one becomes either a forest dweller or an anchoress in these days of vanishing forests and antiquated anchorages?

Back at home, once again on my lanai and still a non-pilgrim, I try to find peace with the fact that the "way" forward is not opening for me.

1 Ward, "The Desert Heart:" wordpress.com

For Such a Time as This

On my sixty-fifth birthday, I sat in a classroom as a "Pastor Scholar" at my alma mater. The professor, now ten years older than at our previous encounter, barely had a gray hair. My own was full of silver strands. This immersion course was meant to explore vocation. A late-life discernment seemed worthy of my time as I eagerly welcomed the forest-dweller idea.

Hinduism describes this transition from householder to forest dweller as the "third stage of life." It is a time for self-realization and retreat from the world. The expectation is to prepare spiritually for the fourth and final phase, when "Spirit" is all there is.

So much had already been decided and settled in sixty-five years of living. There seemed to be little to obscure the view of the horizon. It appeared to me as a vast, wide openness, like a beach windswept after a winter storm. This clean slate signaled a fresh start. Nothing in the prior two-thirds of life needed to be brought forward into this "third life," which lay out ahead in the fullness of time.

The "first day of school" in my sixty-fifth year felt something like the first in my sixth year. I took along my book bag and pens and pencils. While that very first school day was forever emblazoned in my memory for any number of reasons, the first day of being sixty-five was now marked by another classroom. Being the elder in the room felt unexpectedly right; I had already lived a life and had something to say about it. Very early in the morning, my first question, then my second, and so forth surprised me. My voice, my own, my very own, was reverberating like an echo across the years. I wanted to shout and then hear it come back, over and over: "Freedom, freeee, freeee, free ... dom."

On the outside, I imagine I appeared as one might expect an older woman to look. As the week progressed, I saw in retrospect the span of that decade, this gulf that separated me, the student, from me, the independent scholar. It was like a birthday gift received on a late-August day in my sixty-fifth summer. This post-graduate course was supposed to have followed on the heels of my pilgrimage to Norwich. Without becoming a pilgrim, I began to consider the notion of becoming a forest dweller. Not an easy thing in the twenty-first century.

There is no place quite far enough for a forest dweller these days. Living thousands of miles apart from loved ones is akin to being "down the road," while living across the ocean is simply a time-zone issue. Email messages arrive overnight like Santa Claus leaving presents.

I decided to explore being "in the world, but not of the world."

A news moratorium, which I adhered to for six months, certainly detached me in some ways from the world. Functioning with less information makes things simpler, and the simplicity brings less stress. As I became less fettered to what was going on in the world, my attention went elsewhere. But it is not the world of events that a forest dweller must leave, it is the world of those people who most intimately know and encompass him or her.

At age thirty, that need to go out is manifest in a different way than at sixty-five. The young adult steps out of an intimate world into a bigger one. It is a rite of passage that one must take to become a full-fledged adult. Most of us do it in our own time and way, some more gracefully than others. Mine was ugly. I fledged before I had wings with which to fly. There was no turning back, and life took off with me flapping as hard and as fast as I could. By some miracle(s), I made it from one stage to the next. As I move these days through a simpler, quieter transition, I am witnessing my daughter's leap into life. She is not exactly leaping, but cautiously and methodically moving closer, inch by inch, to flying away. It feels painfully slow to me, but at least I know not to push too hard.

My daughter reminds me of the peregrine falcons I watched via webcam high on a parapet above Norwich Cathedral as I prepared for my pilgrimage to England. The three fledglings were completely oblivious to the eyes of the world upon them. At night, they huddled against the wind. The mother came about the same time each day. The fledglings maneuvered as closely to her as possible. Her large, watchful eyes always noticed the smallest chick, pushed to the side by the other two. If necessary, she just tore off another bloody morsel of the carcass from her hunt and placed it into the chick's tiny beak. Then she ate, too. Whenever she was absent, the three hopped about. When their bodies grew larger before the camera's eye, the largest fledglings began hopping again and again up onto the ledge of the parapet. I gasped.

"Don't jump!" I said into the screen. I could see how high they were off the ground. These birds would have a long way to go on their individual maiden flights. Because of the great heights of these nests, medieval falconers who wanted young falcons to train had to capture them on their first flight or migratory pilgrimages. Another name for peregrine falcon is "pilgrim falcon."

One day, I turned on the website after having been absent for some days. The camera was pointed as always on the nest, but it was empty except for the remaining gory mess of leftovers. The fledglings were gone. I felt as if my own offspring had left without saying goodbye.

Soon after, I discovered a recording of the first flights of the fledglings. Each left separately, two fairly close to each other. The smallest left within twenty-four hours of their departure. I watched her (or him) stand on the ledge, eyeballing the situation. She waited. Then suddenly, she leaped with one fell swoop, wings spread wide apart, flapping as if it had all been done before. She was gone. I hoped this little one would make it.

Fledgling falcons and forest dwellers share some commonality—both wander from home and neither can easily be stopped. When the auspicious time appears, one way or another, an inclination moves them forward. There is no return in that decision to go. One simply leaves and does not look back.

Homesickness

Every single trip I have ever taken from as close to home as my native New England to as far away as Thailand, a moment of homesickness has inserted itself. In some moment I feel sad, lonely, wistful for someone or something not present. These days, homesickness has an easy remedy in the myriad forms of technology, a quick fix to take away the sense of strangeness in some place that is not home. The high-tech connection temporarily alleviates the alienation. I recall other times when letters served this purpose, but nothing about that was at all the same.

The most obvious difference is the one-sidedness the writer experiences. The letter leaves one's hand on its own sojourn to some other person and place. The sense of yearning and longing may be so acute in the homebound letter that it borders on heartsickness.

My most memorable homesick moment came in Marrakesh, Morocco. Not one single thing there could be found as a touchstone of home; not even the ubiquitous McDonald's hamburger. There, in this Arabic world of veiled women, I felt completely separate from everyone and everything. I had an eerie sense of having disappeared. This isolation was exacerbated by a male culture that made it unwise and probably unsafe to move around on my own. A woman traveling alone always thinks twice, but it was intensified in this otherwise very hip "imperial city."

One early evening I walked into my tourist hotel. As is the case in many places, drinking the water in Morocco is perilous. Bottled water is the solution, although it brings a whole other set of problems into the country.

Before going upstairs to my room, I remembered I needed to buy a bottle of water. I turned from the lobby toward the hotel bar. I walked into a dark, smoke-filled room of men speaking loudly in Arabic. Before I got to the bartender, I felt two hands on my covered shoulders. The room fell silent. I looked behind me to see a familiar face.

Saiid, a tall tour guide, quietly asked: "Cherie, what do you need?"

"I want a bottle of water for my room," I said in a hushed tone. "Is it OK for me to be in here?"

He looked at the bartender, ordered a liter of cold water, and said, "Let's go."

As I turned to leave, it felt like one giant pair of eyes staring at me in the now silent room. Saiid escorted me to the hotel lobby.

"Is it OK for me to go out on the promenade alone?" I asked.

"Yes, yes, lots of families with children are out there in the evenings. It is very safe. Good night, Cherie."

Later, as I wandered around aimlessly, homesickness crept in, and I wished I was sharing the stroll and the full moon with my own family. Nobody was staring. They just smiled at me, and I smiled back. It did not feel the same years later in Cuba.

As in America, going for ice cream in the evenings in Havana is commonplace.

"Not to be missed," said Adriana, the young tour guide, as we drove by the most-favored ice-cream stand in a park near our hotel.

"Let's go tonight," I said to Arthur.

So, we did. When we arrived at the park, there was a queue that began at the park gates and went on further than we could see. A security guard appeared and asked what we wanted.

"Ice cream," we said.

She pointed us toward the far end of the park, so we walked in that direction, uncertain why we would not line up with everyone else. A second security guard appeared.

"Ice cream?" he asked.

We nodded. He pointed us to a flight of stairs. Again, we obliged.

Upstairs was a small room behind a glass door. Inside were a man behind the counter and one woman on the opposite side. We entered.

The man spoke three words in English, "Vanilla, chocolate, strawberry?"

"Vanilla, por favor," I said.

He scooped silently, then handed it to me. Arthur paid with loose change. The woman licked her strawberry cone. We left with her. She was an Argentinian and had been speaking Spanish with the "Good Humor" ice-cream man. The three of us walked through the park under the watchful eye of the security guard. Once outside the park, we asked the Argentinian:

"What was that about?"

"They want to keep tourists, you Americans especially, out of the crowds of locals."

She crossed a busy street and went her way.

On the one hand, we were glad we did not have to wait in line for our ice cream. On the other, it did not sit well with us that we had been forced into a situation that made us feel like strangers and intruders. Walking along, licking our ice cream, did not make us feel as we had expected it to—as it always had almost anywhere we had ever been. A bit homesick, we decided to return to our government-run tourist hotel and turn in for the night.

In both countries, Morocco and Cuba, the internet access was at best intermittent. In Morocco, when homesickness overtook me, despite the 100-degree midday heat, I put on my long dress and headscarf and walked alone on the main boulevard to a second-floor internet room. I had to wait like the locals and other tourists for a computer. The imposed time limitations and the French keyboard made writing my emails less satisfying than I had hoped. Nonetheless, I felt a little relief from my wistful melancholy when I pressed the *envoyer* button. In Cuba, there was no internet access, even for most Cubans.

"But we find ways," said Adriana, our tour guide, behind closed doors one day in the ladies room.

At one art gallery, we saw Cubans huddled together around old laptops, free "windows" to the outside world that were available there one day a week.

When we were leaving Cuba, Adriana, who was thirty like my own daughter, escorted us into the Havana Airport terminal. I asked this well-educated, bilingual woman a seemingly innocuous question about going through customs.

"I don't know what's on the other side of security, I have never been over there," she said.

Which is worse? I wonder. Not knowing what is beyond one's shoreline, or knowing what one is missing on the other side?

When it comes to homesickness, travel is not a precondition for this type of yearning. Homesickness can be more than just missing "someone" or "someplace." The feelings of yearning can be felt at any time we have "*a strong feeling of wishing for something, especially something that you cannot have or get easily*,"[1] according to one definition. I find this a bit too limited. There can also be a sort of spiritual homesickness for something undefined. It might be described as a sense of not being completely whole. Something is missing.

That homesick feeling has been a prevailing wind blowing through my life, even in childhood. Whether it began before or since the untimely death of my father is unclear. Learning to live without him was my initial experience of loving in absentia.

This experience is not easy to describe. Yet, I doubt it is unfamiliar to anyone who has loved and lost love. In its place, a mysterious connection bridges a deep abyss, an unfathomable canyon, that separates us, one from another. We all yearn for connection. We all live in this world of others like and unlike ourselves. We share resources with all living things, including critters who, like us, require water and air; even the trees, who breathe and provide our source of oxygen. Yet, we often feel alienated, separated, apart from one another, as if in exile. This disconnection makes us feel lonely, in need of connection. That sense of being adrift in the world is the "homesickness" we experience when we are far from the familiar.

1. Cambridge Dictionary

Feeling homesick, this longing for something, can happen anywhere, anytime, even at home with loved ones. It is a sense of separation that I think of as my old friend, melancholy, calling me to the edge of an abyss. I can feel it in the train whistle. I can see it in the falling autumn leaves. I can hear it in a Chopin waltz. I have sung it in a choral requiem. It exists metaphorically and literally in the borderlands, a longing, yearning, homesick feeling that speaks to something missing. We, all of us, have experienced it. Union is what we long for—especially with our Creator.

PART TWO

Borderlands

Big Bend, Texas

The Border Patrol officer asked: "Are you both American citizens?" sticking his own Latino face into the car to get a look at mine.

"Yes," I said emphatically.

We were not crossing any borders. We were on a good old American road trip. Hardly anyone else was on that winding mountain road hugging the Rio Grande River.

My heart was not in my throat when I clearly spoke up, "Yes, I am an American."

What exactly does that mean these days? On that, I am not so clear.

Meandering the far reaches of the Lone Star State, I sang softly to myself, "*America, America, God shed His grace on thee.*"

The sheer beauty and magnitude of these vast valley plateaus, buttes and mesas shone crimson at sunrise and golden at sundown. No other than the hand of the Creator could have carved such magnificence.

The opposite side of the Rio Grande looked identical. Yes, I am an American citizen who lays claim to this side of God's creation. A river separates "us" from "them." Yes, I am an American citizen, but for the grace of God, I would be over on the other border road. If asked that same question there, my answer would have entirely different implications. Who of us asks to be the citizen of the country of our birth? We simply become citizens immediately.

Then at some time, someone asks, "Are you a citizen?"

There is only one answer.

Later that day, standing before a large flat boulder completely covered with handmade trinkets, I stare across the Rio Grande River. Within a stone's throw, on the opposite bank, in the border town of Boquillas, there are Mexicans with voices loud enough to be heard. Both a rowboat and a burro are tied up at the water's edge. When we look across at the Mexicans, I want to wave a "Hello."

Words on the white plastic jug read, *"Boquillas no wall. 10 dollars. Good bless you."* I bend over to pick up one of the wiry figurines of that silly roadrunner bird.

"It is illegal for us to buy these," says a woman holding a chihuahua like a baby in her arms. "It's illegal for them to sell things to us. As soon as you put money in that jar, they'll jump in that boat and come to get it. They've set up camp over there and are watching us." She and her husband, she says, are volunteers, training for work with the Border Patrol.

"They'd risk getting arrested for ten bucks?" I ask, looking across the river, where the laughter is getting louder.

"Yes, sometimes they row over. If the river is low, they walk across. Border Patrol warned us against interacting in any way with them. They come with others to get the money, but you never know how many of them will come."

Listening to her speaking of "them," who appear to be a couple of young men wearing white cowboy hats, I decide I am not willing to take the risk for me or them. Just then, a Border Patrol truck appears and slowly comes toward us. As I walk away, the truck makes a U-turn. I wonder: "Who is the alien? 'Me' on my borderland, or 'them' on their borderland with the Border Patrol in between?"

Lone Star State of Mind

Texans almost wrote a new chapter in the 2018 midterm elections. The "reddest" conservative state with the most on the (border) line held the rest of the country in suspense for a few hours on election night. Could a young, progressive, liberal Democrat unseat the far-right incumbent?

Austin said, "Yes!"

But the tiny towns spread out across the state held the power. Rural means rural in Texas. Hundreds and hundreds of miles as the crow flies between isolated places not only creates distance but insulation. Terlingua is such a place.

This border town is north of the Santa Elena Canyon with its high straight walls split in two by the Rio Grande. One sheer wall is in Texas, the other half, cut off naturally over thousands of years by water running between the two, is in Mexico. Now, that's a border wall!

The "off the grid" house where we spent several nights was a dot in the rugged landscape. We made our way to it not by street signs or any markers, but by incremental measures of our car's odometer.

"At .7 miles, look up over the rise to see the steel roof and wind turbine," said the printed directions, one of many instructions I read out loud to Arthur as we crept ever so slowly over an unpaved, unmarked one-car road. We had made it a point not to arrive after dark.

"There it is." I shouted. The wind turbine spinning around in the gray sky was a welcome sight and the only landmark visible from the road.

The directions for living in the house were just as detailed as the directions for getting there:

> *"If the pump doesn't come on, you may need to put batteries in the hot-water heater. If there is no wind overnight and no electricity in the morning, run the generator for a few hours. The toilet has a toggle switch and foot pedal, turn on the switch first."*

We walked around inside and out, directions in hand, as if on a treasure hunt.

"That looks like a generator," Arthur said.

"Where do you think the hot-water heater is?"

"That's it, I think," I said, pointing to something under the kitchen window. It resembled one at our home inside a closet.

I'm thinking: "We are a long way from Florida here in the remotest part of Texas and the United States."

Rainwater was the only water source, and it was raining. The wind turbine's low humming was the only sound coming from that turning metal apparatus. It was both annoying and comforting.

In the morning, fog enshrouded us. We saw nothing beyond the screen porch for two days except for a tiny Mexican chickadee, which preened itself in the low brush near the house. It was the only moving thing in sight.

The second morning, the wind turbine was not moving, either. I thought this might be a bad thing. Clearly, those solar panels were not generating electricity in the fog. Temperatures were very chilly, but there was no thermometer to tell us how cold it actually was. I wore wool socks and turtleneck sweaters indoors. The pilot light on the gas heater refused to stay lit. I pushed the buttons while Arthur read the sequence of steps:

"Turn the knob while holding down the pilot button . . ."

Suddenly, I lost my temper.

"You do it." I said, defiantly. Equally frustrated, Arthur picked up the car keys from the kitchen table.

"Where are you going to go?" I mocked while escaping by the backdoor onto the porch. Out here, there was no sound and nothing to see in the fog. I drew my shawl up to my neck to ward off the damp rawness of this desert place.

"So, this is what it would be like to live off the grid, to be a forest dweller," I said to myself.

This place in the world, in the universe, was my temporary test. Could I do it? Did I want to? I was remembering a friend who had undertaken this lifestyle when we were in our thirties. I had stayed with her from time to time over the years. That house proved to be more of a burden and less of a joy for her with the passing of time. She reached a point when she felt trapped by the whole liberated lifestyle she had created. I felt myself suddenly standing in her shoes on that back porch in Terlingua. Freedom comes with its price. And two people alone on a rugged mountainside reconcile quickly, we learned.

Sipping tea together in front of the now-lit stove, I said:

"I can see why people living out here do not feel like they need the government."

"That's a significant insight," Arthur replied.

"With all this land and space between neighbors, why would anyone want the government to make decisions for them?" I continued. "I never saw it this way before, but it makes sense, sitting here, doesn't it?"

The fog was beginning to un-cement itself from the ground. There was supposed to be a full moon, but we had yet to see anything in this "dark sky" country. A homemade pot of soup was simmering on the stove and helping to heat the house and us. Then, like a curtain going up on a stage, the heavy mist began to rise across the plateau, revealing an unspeakable panorama of beauty. Words do not work in the face of such majesty. Behind the house was a huge deserted valley. And beyond it, a series of mountain peaks. I held the camera as I turned myself around 360 degrees to capture all of it.

Before the moon rose over the mountains, we discovered the heated outdoor shower. Eureka! As I faced the glowing red mountains, the heated rainwater felt like a blanket over my back. Then, the fading afternoon sun baked the porch and my body. All around us, bright colored birds appeared out of nowhere. Butterflies, too. The flies woke up. And a long-eared jack rabbit bounced by without noticing us.

Those two Mexicans I saw across the river, those two Border Patrol officers we encountered, and the two of us, shared the same borderland. I imagine those young border-control Mexican-Americans, bridging both worlds while maintaining the "law" that keeps us separate, must be living in as much edginess as the two men waiting to cross the river. We, too, felt this edginess. It left an indelible impression of "quiet desperation" deep down inside, like the sound of some goats we heard bleating in the natural beauty of the Santa Elena Canyon. This otherwise lonely "no place" is, in effect, a true place of exile.

Belonging vs Longing

The jack rabbit, the chickadee, the butterflies, and that tarantula tip-toeing across a desert road define a place like Big Bend. An exile's ersatz home may be a remote desert, or forest, or those in-between no places, like the borderlands. They are somewhere in-between Chronos time and Kairos time, like rivers endlessly carving canyons without beginnings or endings.

Here, place is not as important as state of mind. My private push-pull between the active and contemplative life has been like a tug-of-war for decades. I thought I might resolve this internal struggle during my time at Episcopal Divinity School. I discussed it then with a spiritual director. She seemed to be of the mindset that to live a contemplative life would be a very difficult existence. I remember her face registered her own feelings of resistance. In hindsight, she spoke for herself in that moment more than out of concern for me.

In exile, one experiences a certain resistance. One might think of it as pushing or holding back, but the state of resistance is also holding a firm, unequivocal position as in taking a stand or holding one's ground. A firm "No" in the face of a challenging circumstance. Or, an unequivocal "Yes."

"Yes. I am an American citizen."

At that time in my personal life, when divorce proceedings proceeded against my will and my better judgment, my greatest need was to close the door behind me and exist in a tiny campus apartment. It was the antidote to chaos. My place of refuge gave me solitary peace. I listened to the silence and lit candles and incense for long, uninterrupted meditations. I often retreated to write in a backroom sanctuary. Writing in exile is one thing—writing as exile—is entirely another matter.

With the demands of the outside world left at the door, my inner world deepened. The closeness I felt between myself and the Holy did not feel isolating or make me lonely. I knew, as I had when I was a child, that I was never truly alone. To live as a contemplative is not to be a lonely recluse. On the contrary, the life of a contemplative is full. The action within the abode may be minimal, but the activity within the heart is ongoing and lively. It seemed to fit me like a glove.

Exile, the physical place and the interior state, can lead to depths heretofore unknown. Such depths are unfathomable. No wonder we stay as far away as we can from the edge of that abyss.

Tolstoy described it thus in *A Confession*:

> *"I am at a height not just of, say, an extremely tall tower or mountain, but I am at a height such as I could never have imagined. I cannot even discern whether I can see anything there below, in the bottomless abyss over which I am hanging and into which I am being drawn. My heart contracts and I feel terrified."*[2]

Terrified as a child in a dark room alone, the longing within us draws us closer to that immeasurable, unnamable place. Most of all, going there alone is what we are afraid to face. So, we search for someone else to whom and with whom we can belong. Diasporas embark on long journeys together from here to there. Pilgrims often travel together to the sacred sites. The Ark had its pairs who clung together. Adam had Eve when cast into exile. When loneliness is replaced with belonging, something shifts.

Belonging to something, or someone, provides us with what we need to survive our time in exile. Every one of us needs an anchor, be it a person or a place.

The anchorage of Julian of Norwich was attached to a medieval church, my own twelve-by-twelve anchorage is an adjunct to the rest of a Florida townhouse overlooking a river and some railroad

2. Kentish, *Leo Tolstoy, A Confession,* 79.

tracks beyond. I often hear the train whistles. In daylight, I watch the cars rumble past on the tracks. At night, I hear the solemn train whistle calling: "Come, if you want." The longing comes and goes like the trains.

Only a thin mesh screen stands between two worlds, inner and outer. The screened lanai has its boundaries. It feels separate, special, sacred, and enough. I could sacrifice the rest of the house, but not this space. I imagine this space is something like the anchorage of Julian of Norwich in England.

When the full moon rises across the river, everything else ceases to exist for me. Inch by inch, minute by minute, this perfect globe lifts itself like a hot-air balloon casting a long golden wake from one riverbank to the other. Trains may glide by, but the lanai absorbs their evocative call. Oneness enfolds me.

PART THREE

Women Speaking in Exile

The Sweet Spot

The "sweet spot," that place in the center of a tennis racket, never seems big enough. When hit exactly, the ball leaves the racket like a rocket. Finding the sweet spot requires concentration and focus. It means paying attention, regardless of distractions. Meditation masters call this "concentration without effort."

Meditating is like finding the sweet spot during a tennis match. Sometimes it seems impossible. Distractions, small or large, pull attention their way. Learning to limit their impact can take a long time, perhaps a lifetime.

Does one find the sweet spot of one's lifetime in the third life, when the distractions of the world are lessened, or at least seem less important? At long last, where one puts her attention may become a choice rather than a requirement. Women, in particular, wait a long time to find the sweet spot of their lives.

The traditional caregiver role, in most cultures, falls squarely on women's shoulders. That responsibility can become a lifelong endeavor. One reason for this is that those cared for by a woman have a vested interest in preserving her caregiver role. As beneficiaries, it is not in their best interest for women to realize what else they might be called to be. Even one's own mother can be the prohibitor of a daughter becoming fully fledged, fully divested of outlived roles, and, vice versa. What a conundrum.

As a result, women's voices have been less notable in many fields of work and study. Pushed to the margins, their voices sound like cries from the wilderness. Who hears them? Some women use drastic measures to locate their sweet spots and then speak out from that place. Julian of Norwich found her voice in self-imposed exile. Women, like Julian, speak for the other women of their day from their place of exile. We can still hear her speaking to us, in our time.

Did Julian have to go into exile to be heard? Did she need to leave others behind? What price did she pay for leaving? Was it made freely?

The answers are not "one size fits all." There is, however, a universal archetype in each and every story. Women's stories are as "old as the hills," and each one joins at some point the continuum of all stories. All women are part of that continuum, adding our own stories to shared spiritual narratives.

Julian feared that she might forget the visions that changed her life. That fear drove her to write them down. It also moved her, literally, to become the Anchoress of St. Julian's Church, as we know her. That anchorage enclosed her for the rest of her life. Her actual given name is unknown. St. Julian is part of the name of the church where she received "last rites" before she was sealed inside her anchorage. According to the Roman Catholic Church, she was now "dead to the world." The choice to be there was not made lightly.

Julian lived during days when so-called heretics were burned at the stake for having a Bible translated from the church's Latin into English. The Roman Catholic Church was powerfully engaged in village life. Julian found a way to locate herself within the church in order to tell her story in English. Her way was through the anchorage. There she was free to worship and to write with the church's blessing.

Julian committed the balance of her life to writing a full description and interpretation of her earlier visions. She wrote for all people, whom she called her "even-Christians." Julian's many years in the anchorage provided the solitude, time, and privacy required to write her full story and to stay as close as possible to her "one and only," Jesus.

She may have been considered as good as dead, as far as the church was concerned, but exiling herself to this place freed Julian to enter fully into a new prophetic vocation. Living alongside the church's male hierarchy, Julian embraced and sidestepped it simultaneously. Her choice to let go of the outer world gave her a particular freedom to find her own voice within the institution of the church, a most unlikely place for any woman in the Middle Ages.

During her tenure, another role emerged for Julian as village counsellor. Through a window that faced out onto the street, many people stopped to speak with her. They often sought answers to spiritual questions. She was not an official spiritual director, but as a woman, she was clearly way ahead of her time. The anchoress, thought to be on the margins, was actually at the frontier.

Though Lady Julian has not been "sainted" by the Catholic Church, she is held in high esteem as one of its true mystics. Today, both the Catholic and Anglican Church celebrate early May feast days in honor of Julian.

She was a thirty-year-old woman when she experienced her life-changing visions. What is it about that thirty-year benchmark, whether in the Middle Ages or any century, that stands out in bold relief against the rest of one's life, at least for women? As I recall, my hopes and dreams seemed to be all ahead of me. My sense of self, my identity, was tied up with those life dreams that sent me off in many pursuits, too many to accomplish in a lifetime.

My daughter's thirtieth birthday looms ever closer. It is all wrapped up in what her life can, or might, or should be. How can anyone choose? I certainly was no different from Hannah at that age. I knew what I could know through a variety of limited, albeit trying, experiences. Just like her, I had been tested; I failed sometimes and succeeded at others. It came down to expectations of myself and of others, as to whether I was headed in the right direction.

In those early years of becoming a woman, I longed for my father. He might have been a spiritual guide, but I wanted the earthly guy. What would he have offered to me by way of wisdom? I cannot even begin to imagine the myriad ways in which my life might have been different, had he been part of it. The sense of him has been palpable in the way memories sometimes feel real, like the way my six-year-old head rested on his soft belly. It is different for my daughter in these waning years of her twenties because her father has and continues to be an active presence. Except for the years when she was bitterly angry with him for his shortcomings, real and construed, they have shared something I never had beyond the age of eight. When my rite of passage over the thirty-year threshold appeared imminent, I knew I would cross over on my own, like all the other thresholds. For Hannah, her father will be there when she makes her own crossing, God willing. I might feel envious, but how could I?

Fathers can continue to hold their special place in a daughter's heart and life, even as mothers need to separate from their daughters. Having a father present, makes that break-up a little less threatening. The fallback father is witness to mother and daughter cutting the umbilical cord for a second time. Unlike that original cutting, the child will not be immediately placed at her mother's breast. At thirty, that cord-cutting is unceremonious yet life-changing for both. Mothers, while once indispensable, must step aside and away, perhaps into exile.

Julian of Norwich says of her mother in her earliest writing: *"My mother who was standing with others watching me, lifted her hand up to my face to close my eyes, for she thought I was already dead."*[3]

How dramatic for both. Julian lay helpless while the older, wiser woman, was standing as witness to the unthinkable: a dying child. The days of Julian's illness required her mother to nurse her daughter. The adult daughter was crossing death's threshold while her mother looked on. Julian's mother could hardly be a guide under those circumstances. Julian would be going to a place her own mother had not yet seen.

Julian's many visions and experiences, with a present mother and an absent father, may have had some bearing on Julian's own descriptions of those fever-pitched moments, just as living through plague after plague must have influenced her thoughts and beliefs. Julian describes the figure of Jesus as *"Mother-Jesus."* She speaks of this Mother-Jesus in terms of endearment, *"dear mother love."* She describes Jesus as a mother who *"Succors us at the breast. Feeding us with himself."* Motherhood, Julian says, *". . . provides wisdom and knowing, is kindly, loving and tender.*[4]

3 Spearing, *Revelations of Divine Love*, 66.

4. Spearing, *Revelations of Divine Love*, 142.

The description of her mother at her deathbed is in her original writing, *A Vision Showed to a Devout Woman* often called her Short Text. Julian wrote those sixteen showings soon after her recovery from her near-death experience. In her longer text, written while in exile in the anchorage more than twenty years later, Julian had broken away from her own mother. Here, she exclusively describes Jesus as "Mother."

Julian's illness did not result in her crossing the threshold called death, but it marked her own transformation from Julian the daughter to Julian the mystical woman. At some point after her illness, she was no longer so attached to her role as daughter or to her earthly mother. She stood on the other side of that divide, free to choose to become an anchoress and live out her life in self-imposed exile.

For Julian, as for many of us, the horizon line moved from prospective to introspective like a vanishing point between before and after. That horizon line is not fixed but is a moveable goal post. In the sports world that might be an egregious breach of the rules. Yet in life, getting to that goal of crossing over the proverbial threshold is change itself. Life circumstances are often the catalyst.

When outer change comes in any form, birth and death being the two biggest, one must change. Some may prefer the status quo to change. But try as one might, the inevitable change will come. If it comes from the inside out, the result is more than change. It is transformation.

Julian, in her life-changing visions, exemplifies this before-and-after effect. Julian at thirty, lying on her deathbed, was a relatively small self. Her greatness was to be found through her metaphorical death: She gave it all up, left it all behind her.

Everyone familiar with Julian's life story has been told we know very little about her early life, including her real name. How apropos. Julian emerged at the age of fifty as an anchoress. From that point on, we know her full story, living as she did, alone at the frontier, assuming the spiritual guide's role as simply and quietly as a church mouse. How remarkable that such a story should have survived six centuries while continuing to grow in popularity.

Hers is a classic mother-daughter story in which daughters leave their mothers. In that regard, Julian and her mother were no different in the Middle Ages than we are today. At least for a while, one cannot remain part of that powerful mother-daughter duo and make the needed change. It is impossible. Mothers ought to see this inevitability from the moment the umbilical cord is severed at birth. That symbiosis begins to end at the start. Whoever creates the change within this relationship forges the way for both. As daughters, we depart from the "homely" mother, Julian's way of speaking about Jesus as "Mother," who creates a loving home for us all.

Julian of Norwich forged her own frontier through self-imposed exile in the Middle Ages. Many other spiritual stories of women have been buried simply because, as women, they were never taught to read or write. They deserve to be unearthed, like the story of Julian. As a woman living beyond the traditional norms, she wrote to and for all women across all centuries, speaking out in exile.

Name Dropping

All the years Hannah was in school, including college, I introduced myself as "Hannah's mom." It felt natural. I was proud to be the mother of that person on the balance beam, in the swimming pool, up on horseback, on the basketball court, at the potter's wheel, behind the camera, at the piano, and especially when she received awards and diplomas.

When she was little and throwing a tantrum in the mall stores, I felt like disappearing into the clothes racks. When she faltered in high school competitions before her peers, I huddled with her rather than holding her. She had outgrown the public display of motherly affection.

At home, we sat for extended chats on the sunny patch of the kitchen floor or by the fire with hot cocoa. On trips to her college campus, we had to make do with restaurants and cafes or walks together to talk in the way we had become accustomed.

Throughout her life, whenever and wherever I could, I intervened from behind the scenes with calls to teachers, emails to other parents, texts to friends and boyfriends—all from "Hannah's mom." That was me: defined and summed up in two words. One of those words was her name, not mine. In using her first name rather than my own, I usurped something of myself and stole something from her. The adult in our single-parent household had left the room, as it were. "Hannah's mom," however, was ever present. She and I had become appendages of one another. No wonder each of her attempts to leave home has proved so painful for her. A series of steps forward, then back, is the pattern she now means to break. For her to leave home, we two must "break up" and each of us knows "breaking up is hard to do."

One would think that by moving 1,000 miles away from her that we had already done so. Yet, distance creates a different dependency. Without regular time to be together, lengthy phone calls substitute for face-to-face chats. We save it up and then talk for hours at a time, often until one or the other of our phones goes dead. Not so surprisingly, the scales are tipping as she approaches her thirtieth birthday. It has taken us that long. The first noticeable fault line in our relationship appeared a few years ago when I gave her my "special" Christmas present:

"Pick any weekend you want for our mother-daughter weekend and I will make the reservations and book my flight to Boston." I thought she needed this. Therefore, I would travel north in winter, leaving my warm tropical climate to do so.

As if I had used a pickaxe, the ice cracking could be heard from Cape Cod down to Florida. I had backed her into something she did not want, let alone need, at the time. Of all the things for her to have to push back on; I thought our mother-daughter weekends were sacrosanct.

"I can't even get a weekend with my boyfriend," she said, balking over the phone.

"Hannah's mom" was not who she wanted or needed me to be anymore. "Hannah's mom" was stopped in her mama-bear tracks. "Hannah's mom" shed some tears of sorrow for herself, although she knew, like those peregrine falcons, that the auspicious time had come for mother and chick to fully fledge and not look back.

Heartstrings

Is this about my daughter or me? Are the two of us jumping into our own different worlds? She, the thirty-year-old fledgling, me the aspiring forest dweller? She, the woman embarking on a life; me just embarking. Two ends of the same string: Heartstrings.

Hannah's preschool singing group was named "Heartstrings." She has had my heart on a string for twenty-nine years plus nine months. Time, often, seemed not to move. Would she ever grow up? Would I ever be free from mothering? Yes, is the answer to both—Yes. Of course, it was always a foregone conclusion that she and I would reach this moment of departing, one from the other, separately taking off. I had anticipated this prematurely when she went to college. I was ready. It was what we had been moving towards together for years.

"Do you think I'm ready?" she sobbed days before leaving home for college.

"Yes, you are," I said with full authority, heart in throat. She seemed so vulnerable and so young. If I had said "No," would it have been so wrong? It perhaps would have been more truthful. We both took a step toward separate lives in that mother-daughter conversation. Separate, but not apart, yet. A decade hence, the true separation is finally upon us.

The intervening years have been a series of separations. She, moving around the country—to Maine, to New York City, then back to Cape Cod; me to Boston, then to St. Augustine. She is making a new world for herself as she explores the bigger world through travel. We both have "travel fever." It started when she was five years old. Each winter school vacation, because her father's work prevented our taking a family vacation, the two of us would go away on a short trip together. There have been twenty-plus mother-daughter weekend trips. Our most recent was the longest, but not one either of us anticipated taking together. It was, after all, to be her road trip.

The centennial celebration of the U. S. National Parks brought her travel fever to a pitch. Her sense of adventure and need to escape from a drifting, post-college life stirred in her the need to go. At every stage of the methodical planning process for her six-week trip, I lived vicariously through phone calls and emails. She and her then boyfriend, who proved to be very much still a boy, were the travelers. She must have known inwardly that I would have said "yes" to this trip at any moment. That moment came when, increasingly, her travel companion was waffling within his own insecurities. When the two arrived on our Florida doorstep, where the road trip was to begin, the whole thing started to sputter. Day after day, their departure was pushed back.

"Maybe tomorrow would be better."

It took Hurricane Matthew and our evacuation order to get them on the road. We were all forced out together, in separate cars, but in tandem. Arthur and I wondered if they would go on their way now? I sensed a "now or never" moment reminiscent of her departure for college.

"You're ready to go—car packed, maps—time is fleeting. Bon voyage," I said, as Hannah wiped tears from her face. I held back my own until she drove away and was out of sight. Arthur and I waved as they drove off to the west, then we turned back east to assess the aftermath of the hurricane.

"Parting is such sweet sorrow," I thought, "but bittersweet."

Then came Christina. She is the first of three grandchildren to fledge. Another hurricane dovetailed with her departure from home two weeks after graduating from high school, just like I had done when I was barely eighteen years old. One minute we were witnessing the first grandchild marching in high heels and royal-blue cap and gown, the next she was leaving the purple walls of her childhood bedroom. She now lives three hours from home. A major Category Four hurricane was soon barreling toward her. A newly minted college freshman, living with roommates, her parents recommended "sheltering in place."

My only son, her father, told me: "She's a native Floridian who has witnessed these things all her life. She knows what to do."

Witnessing is the operative word in my mind. The "witness" is not the victim. One may feel emotionally like a victim when a witness, but the two are different as night and day. Hurricane Michael was headed right for her dorm room decorated with childhood memorabilia. Fledged? Time will tell. At Christina's age, I walked down the aisle. Inside, silently, my heart was screaming "Stop."

My mother played her mother-of-the-bride role perfectly, if not reluctantly. Her own heart must have been screaming, too. The church organist ought to have played horror-movie music, not "Oh Promise Me." The innocent victim came on the scene a year later wrapped in a blue blanket. The two-year marriage was frightful and fraught from the very beginning. Soon, I was a single mother, like my own mother. Fully fledged. No turning back.

I have always viewed my young adult life in juxtaposition to my mother's. She settled for a dreary daily existence, while I ran as fast as I could to escape it. Because of that dichotomy, it was impossible to forget her seemingly joyless life as I pursued a life of my own. It was as if our fates were inextricably tied together. Wherever I went, or whatever I did to escape, she was there in my mind.

Standing now on the forest-dweller ledge, I have all the advantages of perspective. Moments come in subtle waves of peace and joy—not joyfulness—simpler than that—best described as calm contentment. Whenever my mother used the words "being content" to speak about her own life, I balked.

Content? Why would anyone settle for being content?

She had, to my young eyes, caved to the circumstance life had thrown at her with mighty force. I wanted more for her. Within that, of course, was a whole wad of wishes for a life completely different from hers.

Woman at the Well

I can remember when this happened to me. It was a time before some of the key people who have filled up my life entered into it. It might have been the beginning of me meeting "me." The day itself was rather ordinary, but because it is alive in memory, it is extraordinary. My age at the time is irrelevant, but the timeframe puts me somewhere shy of thirty. I think of it now as a moment different from all the rest in my life, appearing now as a shadow on the wall of my life story, sometimes seen, sometimes not. At that moment, I was completely free from anyone's expectations. I was simply me on my solitary path.

Standing in the aisles of a busy bookstore in the Philosophy and Religion section, I was unaware of the opening of a door in my "self." It was not a door to *my* self; it was a door inviting and drawing me into the many, many unknowns beyond my present self. It did not open with a creaking sound, but rather, silently. It was unlocked for me from the other side by an invisible hand. At that moment, I stood holding some book that spoke to another self. The chaos of Harvard Square swirling all around disappeared from my sensory perceptions. As though I were standing alone in a quiet, peaceful cemetery of innumerable stories on stones, the books all around were themselves doors into another realm. An entry into "being" on another plane.

"Come hither," a silent voice said, calling secretly right in the middle of the kerfuffle of the bookstore.

A "silent voice?" How can that be? The invitation to step away from the bustle is still clear to me. That was a crossing over the threshold moment. That was a timeless space. That was a limitless dimension. That was a time-stopping experience. That was the proverbial "narrow gate." I entered briefly, but what I found there I cannot say. I recall, shortly thereafter, signing up for my first course in philosophy. It was a first step.

Within a few weeks, I realized I should have chosen a religion course. I quit. The next opportunity would not come for another twenty years, when I entered divinity school at age fifty. I sense an uncanny connection to Julian's timeline of making huge decisions at thirty and at fifty years of age. Like her, I lived fully in the world during the intervening years with that silent voice only barely audible through daily noise. Nonetheless, that voice had made an indelible impression on my interior world.

I often tried to clear some space in my busy family life to make room for the voice. I made occasional solo retreats, attended church weekly, and organized spiritual book-reading groups at my church. But, the true sense of that other realm seemed to disappear into the din. I spent little time looking for it. Catching sight of a falling star or a serene sunset would remind me once again. I took note of those quiet revelations momentarily, before my attention would be drawn to someone or something that was needing me. I needed, too.

It was easy to fill my need for love and caring with those around me, but not so easy during busy days to hear that summons, that quiet call. One day, while sitting by myself, reading the newspaper, something similar happened:

I was no longer actually reading, though I held up the newspaper with both hands in front of my eyes. As in the bookstore years earlier, there came an unsolicited awareness of another realm. In that brief moment, I understood "everything," as if all the answers to all the questions registered at once. Crystal-clear knowledge appeared in a split second, and I saw, momentarily, Jesus on the Cross. As if the flash on a camera had gone off, "poof" it was just as suddenly gone again. As I reconnected with the newspaper, I wondered what had happened in that little room where we liked to watch TV. I tried to recreate the experience mentally. I tried to recall what "all the answers" were, but like a dream, it dissipated. Who in the world could understand such an experience?

When I found myself sitting beside Reverend Jim at a meditation, I asked in hushed tones: "Has this ever happened to you?"

Looking into the clearest, bluest eyes I have ever seen, I "heard" his unequivocal "Yes" in the nod of a head.

My mind's eye bridges the gap between then and now. Before-and-after snapshots flicker when I close my eyes. She/I had stepped into the void, into the eternal, into the limitless, twice. Without those experiences, those memories, there might be no interior story to tell. Without that encounter with the existential eternal, the void, the limitless, there is no depth, no core, no connection to the Source, without which there is no true "me."

What if I could have stayed there on that illimitable threshold? If I had, a few things are certain. My life would have been entirely different. I would not have known some of the key people who were to become part of my life story. Speculation about a different life is as fruitless as speculating about the stock market. The only certainty in both cases is that ups and downs will be part of the story.

As a full-fledged adult on yet another threshold, standing in a more deliberate stance, I have been watching and waiting for the door to that other realm to be opened for me, again. As I have reluctantly faced other doors closing in my life, I have meditated, imagining those doors left ajar to be easily opened rather than firmly shut. I prayed, if and when lost loves had a change of heart, it would be easy to blow down the door with one breath. I hoped against hope. Simultaneously and unbeknownst to me, while I held open doors for loved ones to walk through, that door to the other realm was opening for me. I stood on that in-between threshold for what seemed like an eternity, afraid to make a move. Then, I took a step toward the one and only true me—into another realm.

After that, my face had turned toward home, and there was no turning back. The "in betweenness" feels different now. It is somewhere beyond a borderland. This beingness is nondescript, like some vast openness. The immensity is all-encompassing. Passing from some borderland to in-betweenness is like coming out of the proverbial desert. It reminds me of that first encounter with my "self." I had glimpsed her then and came face to face with her thirty years hence.

Those rare jewels, those moments in time, glimmer in hindsight. I had been placed squarely on the edge of or within the limitless void. Those moments might have been turning points. But, like the Rio Grande borderland, the turning is not at right angles or 180 degrees in another direction. The river of life, like all rivers, meanders and curves itself around the surrounding landscape. It does not abruptly change from one direction to another. Rather, it follows its own natural way.

Water always finds a way. I, too, followed many twists and turns without knowing where they would lead. It was not as clear, looking outward, as it is now, looking backward.

Every turning moment has moved me toward and away from some other, except at that deepest place. At the depth of the well, "All" met me, and I met "It," briefly, but eternally. Is it possible to return to those moments? To "step into the same river twice?" Is it possible to create moments of the eternal? Must a crisis precipitate the threshold moment? Are we free to go there? Stand there? Stay there? Is this the call the forest dweller must heed? Is this the way the anchoress enters the anchorage?

An Anchoress in the Making

The key defining moment of my life was the death of my father, when I was a child. Loss, sorrow, loneliness ensued and colored my early years. I knew no other person my age who could be simpatico. Sitting alone, in the dark, up close to the black-and-white television screen, I watched the befuddled, bespectacled, cartoon character, Mr. Magoo, who sang to me from his own loneliness:

"Where is the hand that claps to my hand? Where is the heel that clicks to my clack? I'm all alone in the world."

That Mr. Magoo was a cartoon character did not matter one bit to me at that moment. I knew he knew.

To remember such poignant loss and loneliness and to have never shared it with anyone but Mr. Magoo made it a secret of my heart. The solitariness in that memory is the very thread that connects me with each and every soul, linking us together in the most profound way. Julian of Norwich is as linked to my story as I am to hers. She overrode the solitariness of her anchorage by being in complete "One-ness" with the Divine. Her story, though ancient and archaic, is universal. That is a bold statement, yet it is an understatement.

Julian stands out because she shared her most secret sacred moments, making them manifest. Each of us has some of these same moments within us. She articulated the invisible. She knew the fullness of the Divine had been revealed to her in her loneliest, dying days. She experienced another realm, which gave her that proverbial gift of eternal hope, as expressed through undying words: *"All shall be well."*[5]

That hope, which she passed on to her peers, is now reaching us across the ages. She knew that her life, like all of ours, had to come to terms with this truth that no matter how alone we are in the world, we are never truly alone. She locked herself securely into the one place where she felt sure she could hold on to that truth for her lifetime, while sharing it with those who witnessed her life and with many of those who would not. She relished her visions and reveled in them long afterward. Without her writing, these extraordinary gifts would have disappeared in the fourteenth century along with her. Her manuscript was saved by others, who knew its present and future value. The story she wrote enters into our own stories as one universal story we all can share.

The eight-year-old me, alone with the TV knew nothing of Julian, nothing of England; but I did know about being "all alone in the world." By divine grace, (via Mr. Magoo), I had the sense of not being the only one who knew this feeling. There was someone else. One does not feel so "all alone," if one knows there is someone else who feels it, too. This truth saved and sustained me. Not being "all alone," when our outer reality disappears, means there must be, has to be, another realm, an invisible other that connects the two, like the mystic Julian connecting across six centuries with Mr. Magoo.

5. Spearing, *Revelations of Divine Love*, 22.

Cherishables

Closing my eyes allows a time machine to take me over many decades of memories of the myriad places and people I have encountered. Hit the pause button, and pages open up to particular places in my mind: my bedroom shared with sisters; screened-porch sleepovers on summer nights; backyard swings shared with cousins; city-bus strangers on the way to school; railroad tracks where teenage friends smoked stolen cigarettes; that middle pew of St. Marie's every Sunday morning with my family.

In my memory, music has its own special place. Songs take me to the high-school cafeteria where I met, for the first time, our chorus director, Mr. Filiatro, perpetually wearing his dark bow tie. That same space on Friday nights, was transformed from our boring student lunch lines to dancing lines, as we strutted in too-high heels.

In hindsight, it seems I was rarely on my own except in my cherished tree in the woods behind my house. There, only, I would sit and take stock of family injustices and expectations. The tree did not know me by name. It knew the "me" I meant to be but failed to be so often. Miles of trees between then and this third life do not obliterate my view in hindsight. Some rare instances stand out taller as do some trees.

This "me," was hardly known to myself, and not at all to anyone else. She was the solitary ice skater after school on the pond; the young girl at the piano after father died; the adult late at night in the library; the woman walking on the winter beach; the writer at her desk at dawn; the one on the lanai at sunrise. Had she been preparing all her life to be a solitary anchoress? Nobody would have believed it.

"She's a social butterfly," mother whined to anyone who would listen.

The label stuck and had unintended consequences. It was something to live up to, even if I did not aspire to it. It became a burden to bear on my five-foot frame. In the confines of that socially acceptable role, I could barely breathe. I learned only to exhale, to put it all out there for the world to see, to test and evaluate, then to admire or reject me. The roles I adopted throughout my life prove out the facts of this existence. I maneuvered through my life with borrowed wings. I managed until I could no longer. Mostly, what stopped me in my tracks came at me like a freight train. When circumstances derailed my adult life, the choice to change my "self" became mine at long last. I could have stayed on my well-worn path. After all, that was what was expected of a mid-life woman and mother. Instead, I stepped off the path altogether. I stepped away from these roles and into my "self," the one I met one day as a young woman long ago in the Harvard Coop bookstore.

Missing Person

When I graduated from divinity school, I was not included in my class photo, taken in May 2008. I was, to be sure, present and "hooded" in front of my classmates, my son and daughter, ex-husband, new lover, and close friends. It was a moment I had only imagined most of my life. Waiting had meant many years of sacrificing one thing for another. The compromises made throughout a lifetime of mothering included forgoing this dream until I was in my fifties. While I had never planned to go to divinity school, here I was, after three years of study, collecting my diploma. Yes, certainly I appreciated it all the more. Yes, I was a more mature student. Yes, I earned every grade and paid every cent of tuition myself. At long last, on that day of days, surrounded by family and friends, my heart overflowed.

My son, Peter, had come from his home elsewhere in Florida. My high-school-aged daughter took off from school and drove the two hours up, then back, despite her first-ever art show opening on the very same day. We were like a well-oiled machine going from my graduation to her opening—endings and beginnings tied up with one blue ribbon.

Just as soon as my graduation had spilled out onto the Cambridge sidewalk, we all hurried to our cars to get down to the Cape Cod Art Museum.

One of my professors called out: "They're about to take the class photo. You're going to miss it."

"I know," I said without stopping, looking behind as I hurried, seeing both our black gowns unzipped and billowing in the May breeze.

That class photo of my cohorts registers me as absent, a missing person.

Recently, I came across it in a red box on a closet shelf. I had placed the official photo there with the diploma and white and red polyester hood. With a blue marker, I had written on top of the box *"GRADUATION."* Looking at the photo of familiar, friendly faces smiling towards the future brings it all back.

I see Christi and Sandi, both women my age with families of their own, plus Hall, so tall he stood out in the back row. I am reminded of his guitar-playing moments in the quad. In their faces, I recognize their stories. Each had sacrificed something to pursue this particular dream toward a different life. My missing face spoke to my own life, fixed as it was in the same old place at that moment.

Nobody but me can insert a mental placeholder into that picture where I would have been, most likely in the front row, as I had been in all previous class photos. The missed photo opportunity spoke to my future having to wait a little while longer.

Meanwhile, back on Cape Cod on that loveliest of May days, I stood in a different photo with my daughter in front of her wonderful works of art. How pleased we felt in that moment is all over our faces. I felt no regrets, just pride at being there beside her, where I belonged.

The photo, like all photos, stirs nostalgia with a silver spoon.

"That seems like a long time ago, doesn't it?" said Arthur, peering over my shoulder at the photo. It is a fond memory, a starting point in our own story. As I re-packed the photo, I wondered what ambitions still remain? Who in my life belongs? Where do I belong? That is the biggest question of all.

Who Was that Woman at the Well?

Staying too long—at a party, at a friend's home, or with one's own children—is a recipe for disaster. The last partygoer bears the brunt of being discussed later by others; over-staying as a houseguest will be long remembered; and parenting beyond the "legal" age invites dependency, the archenemy of motherhood.

"You are the bows from which your children as living arrows are sent forth,"[1] wrote the prophet Kahlil Gibran.

Sending them forth is the main goal of parenting. That means raising them up to go out and contribute something, somewhere. When mothers prevent that going forth by prolonging dependency, it is a failure for both mother and child. It is strange that I never saw it before my daughter pointed it out to me. It took her needing to be free from her mother, me, before I saw clearly how detrimental maternal love can be when coddling continues into young adulthood. Thank God, she saw it, named it, and spoke her truth.

In getting herself free, she set me free. I don't know if I would have had the courage or the will to stop being "Hannah's mom." Relinquishing my key identity was a prerequisite for growth. Hannah no longer wishes to be my little girl, so she can grow into adulthood. I, her mother, need to close the book, finally, on an identity I assumed from the start of my own adulthood, when I became a mother before growing into full adulthood myself.

1. Gibran, *The Prophet.*

I honored my motherhood more than my own mother's. She could seem so elusive, often saying: "I cannot be both your mother and your friend," most often it seemed when I needed a friend. I have over-compensated with my own children.

While single parenting my son, we rode bikes together, taught ourselves to play chess, and saw all the *Star Wars* movies together. I called him "my little man" when I had no man of my own. Years later, when my daughter was born, her father became a second-class citizen in the household. I turned toward her fully and stood with her against the whole world. I owned that identity with all my heart and mind. She pushed back as a teenager, as I had, and as all teens do. I chalked it up to her rite of passage, while forgetting that I had to cross my own threshold for us to be truly free.

When my son departed at puberty to live with his father, a threshold moment was forced upon me. I later indulged my daughter far too long, preventing us both from crossing over. College ought to have naturally separated us, but I deliberately lived within a three-hour drive from her campus, precluding our true separation.

When she struggled as a freshman, I took her to lunch—three hours up—three hours back. I offered her love from home in regularly mailed care packages. I rushed to the scene when she called in times of distress. All the while, my new husband of a few months, waited patiently on the sidelines for this woman whose motherly love was all-consuming. At college graduation, we let out a collective sigh of relief. It was premature.

For my daughter, the ensuing post-college years were full of the stresses of adjusting to the adult world. Mother was on standby for long, long phone calls that could neither be cut short nor interrupted. The message was clear: I am here if you need me; and, because you are calling, you must need me.

Trying to break free of some of the more potent expectations, like holidays, I travelled. But, as we all have come to realize in the twenty-first century, there is always a way to stay connected, no matter where we go, or do not, as is the case in a pandemic. Hannah and I Skyped from Italy, Spain, and China (although the China video was blocked). The next step was to move to Florida. It was the long-awaited inevitability of the decision I had made fifteen years earlier. As it turned out, I did not yet see this as the beginning of my self-imposed exile. I was simply following through with that choice made during my divorce. The transition was not a clean break.

A thousand miles is a three-hour non-stop flight. Easy-peasy. Too often, I made a quick trip north, whenever a few months passed without seeing Hannah. In doing so, I was not setting her or me free. She refused to Skype for the same reason I wanted to, i.e., to look into her eyes. How sad that her blueberry eyes had to turn away as if from a predator. It seems I missed all the clues. All of them.

Whenever I heard pain, I responded. If I felt her fear, I jumped in; if I sensed anxiety, I denied it. Denied her very truth in that moment! How will she ever find it in her heart to forgive me? I am not crying for myself. I am beyond self-pity at this stage of my growth. I am sad for us. We once shared a preciousness that was much more fragile than I realized. Hearts are like that. I should have learned that by now.

Quakers speak about *"holding someone in the Light."* I have meditated these last months on holding Hannah in the Light. It brings to memory her first Christmas Eve, when Hannah was five months old. She was bundled up in a bright-red snow suit.

When we entered the church, Reverend Jim approached us. "Hannah will be the youngest baby here tonight. Would you like to help her to light the first candle?"

This age-old candle-lighting service has been repeated since the 1600s in this Sea Captain's church on Cape Cod. From the youngest to the eldest, the light is passed before it goes into the entire congregation row by row. The pews were always packed. We might have been setting up a fire trap, but that did not stop anyone from cramming into that sacred wooden place for this celebration.

The church fell silent and dark. I walked carefully with Hannah in my arms to the front, where the large red-pillar candle was burning brightly. I extended her arm in mine as I held a tapered candle to the "Light of the World." The two candles became one in the fire before I moved our candle away from the source. I was holding her in the Light. My sense of that candle-lighting, where we were one with the light, still burns deeply in my heart. It is a light that cannot be extinguished, no matter what.

One Christmas, not so long ago, my daughter gave me a white agate heart-shaped stone from Morocco. She also got one for herself so we would "each have one to hold." Often when I sit at my desk, I see the stone sitting there. Instinctively, I hold it, turning it round and round. It feels smooth. It gets warmer and warmer as I rub it gently with my thumb. It is shiny, not transparent but translucent. Even when holding it up to the light, I cannot see through it, but these two stone hearts allow light to pass through them. This is the truth about love—not only motherly love:

All love masks the flaws in ourselves while still allowing the light to shine through.

Can this woman who stayed too long at the well of motherhood have failed herself? Her daughter and son? My eyes drop down to a note on my desk, given to me by another woman, a mother. I read what has been staring me in the face all along: "*Love never fails.*"

Women and Daughters

For Hannah and me, walking the edge of the abyss these past six months has threatened our future mother-daughter relationship.

Standing there, on the lip of the well, looking into that unfathomable void, I could see the empty spaces left by the parents I once needed, the lover I lost, and the friendships I let go. Those compound losses cannot add up to what might have become the greatest of all, the loss of my only daughter's love. But we both stepped back from that abyss in the nick of time.

Listening to an old friend's story about her daughter no longer speaking to her has reminded me of a long-past decade of silence between me and my mother. As my friend talked, I thought to myself how deeply I must have hurt my mother. Fortunately, shortly before she died, I apologized for all I had done or not done and forgave her for the same, setting us both free.

While visiting a friend's house, morning phone calls from her daughter on the West Coast seemed to be a harbinger of my future with Hannah. Someday, we may talk as she walks to work in the city or nurses an infant at her own breasts. Time, in this regard, is on our side.

In the meantime, I grow in understanding of how one "lets go" of those most loved. According to a Buddhist monk seated in his scarlet robe at a meditation I attended, this act of "letting go" is "freeing" for all parties. Letting go at the right moment is as important as the actual letting go, if not more so. Like helping a toddler learn to take small steps or a child to ride a bicycle, there will be an auspicious time to drop the guiding hand.

Letting go within a mother-daughter relationship seems less obvious, at least to me. A premature letting go, by either party, will feel like abandonment, the antithesis of "freeing." Only the one who leaves will feel free under those circumstances, leaving little choice for the one who is left. I knew my long marriage was over the day I finally saw that he had given up. Nothing, I realized, would change that fact. When I finally saw it, I let go. The struggle and the marriage were over.

My daughter and I are practicing our high-wire act of letting go without a safety net. Some days, Hannah takes away her hand from mine. Other days, I release hers. I sense our mutual needs in this delicate dance. The auspicious time is upon us.

It is not only that she is moving closer and closer to being thirty, or that I am far away geographically. These are by-products. We have come to the time in our individual lives when separation spells growth for both of us. Neither will grow or change properly, if we maintain the status quo.

Just as I knew when her dad had "thrown in the towel," I clearly see in hindsight that this moment with Hannah was foretold a few years ago. I ignored that sign and perhaps others, too. One scene plays like a movie in my mind. That April, I had traveled up the Eastern seaboard from St. Augustine to the fishing village of New Bedford for her post-baccalaureate art exhibit.

The show was a success in all ways. Afterward, Hannah, her cohorts, and professors, were gathered in the university gallery. The wine flowed. As the evening wound down, Hannah announced her plans to go out with friends to celebrate while handing me the key to her apartment, where I would spend the night. I asked someone where I might find something to eat. I was told of a diner that sold good soup. Perfect for a frigid, snowy, early spring evening in New England.

I laid down my wet scarf and gloves in a booth by the window. As I sat alone, waiting for my meal, I caught my reflection in the glass. My hat and turned-up collar framed my face, looking back at me like a certain Edward Hopper painting. I was that woman sitting alone in a diner in a deserted town on a cold night.

"How did this happen?" I wondered.

I did not begrudge my daughter and her friends partying. I wanted her to share this special moment with them, knowing that without them I would have been her default companion; not good for either of us. But, on this night, she did not stop to think about me, any more than when she had taken her first steps at ten-months-old or had pedaled the bike on her own at age ten. Each time, as on this evening, she was moving away from me towards her own new world. She is growing up and away.

Recalling Hopper's depiction of that woman seated in a diner was art imitating life, my life. The woman seated alone in the painting appears to be abandoned, but maybe there is more to the story than meets the eye. Just maybe, that woman sitting alone, is practicing "letting go" of someone she loves.

222,000 Miles from Home

January 2019

A full winter "wolf" moon ensconced itself in a pinkish-orange shawl borrowed from Mother Earth. It hung at midnight like a perfect ornament in a dark sea of celestial glitter. This full eclipse, lasting one hour and overlapping two dates on the calendar: January 20 and 21, 2019, would be the last of its kind for two years. "It was traditionally believed that wolves howled due to hunger during winter, according to *The Old Farmer's Almanac.*[1] Wolves are lonely looking creatures. We humans project that on them. Yet, they travel together in packs. When one howls, "ah oooh," it is calling out to find the pack, "Where are yooooouh?" Nothing eerie about that. Each of us knows that feeling of being lost, exiled, and calling out for others. During the eclipse, I could hear in the distance neighborhood dogs barking in unison.

The cold, clear air filled my nose with memories of standing under other full moons in frigid temperatures. In the Sunshine State, such a sensation comes rarely, just like that "supermoon, blood, wolf moon." Without a telescope, I craned my neck to look straight overhead.

A few months earlier, at the MacDonald Observatory atop a mountain near Fort Davis, Texas, a full "hunter" moon came close as could be through a large telescope. How was it possible that I

---

1. Boeckmann, Watch for January's Full Wolf Moon.

could be seeing this, in the far-off distance, with my own eyes? It seemed to be a miracle. As is my habit, I offered up a few prayerful thoughts of gratitude for such majesty made visible. I talked, as I so often do, to Great Spirit whenever I see something of Itself shown to the weary world. In the silent stillness, I sensed One-ness with One, so near and yet so far away. I saw craters on the moon's surface. And it seemed impossible to me that three human beings had once walked there, about 222,000 miles away from home.

One of those astronauts said in retrospect that his experience, shared then by only two others in the history of humankind, created within him a deep loneliness. He was living in a kind of exiled state on Earth, unable to share his "out of this world" experience with anyone, including his wife. What might the wonder and awe of an eclipse evoke for him?

For me, besides stirring some memories of other eclipses, I sensed a somewhat distant yet heartfelt connection. The moon above me was suspended in its own rightful orbit, mesmerizing millions of people like me, standing below it from the U.S. to the U.K. But, unlike the solitary astronauts, we stood in solidarity in varying degrees of dress, watching and waiting together while sharing this common experience. It was a free gift from the universe.

As my hands got colder, the fullness of the shadow moved ever so slowly. It did not turn black like a shadow, but pastel. I saw a few neighbors run out from their houses to catch a glimpse and a quick cellphone photo. They stayed only a minute. I wanted more than that one hour. I thought, if a "rock star" had been passing by instead of our moon, throngs would be standing here to see, no matter how long it took. Natural wonders so often go unnoticed and unobserved. Why is that? Maybe we have not been taught to look and see. One day in a cafe, I overheard a mother trying to teach her son about the sky from his science textbook. He could not seem to understand the solar system and its organization of planets. Increasingly frustrated, his mother pushed the book over to his side of the table.

"Read it again until you see what I mean," she said.

I wanted to say, "Go outside tonight and look up." The book was static, but the sky is full of life.

In the morning after the eclipse, remembering my sense of One-ness brought a few tears. I missed my daughter's being there. I had so wished at that moment to be sharing what we had seen together in the starlit sky in previous years. I made a wish and offered a silent hopeful prayer that we might still have other times to share such moments together. I offered my prayer, burned incense to Great Spirit, and thought to myself, "I will watch and wait for a sign that my prayer has been heard and accepted." Soon thereafter, I read that Great Spirit is another name for this January full moon.

Surrendering

My little chick flew first. Me, her "mama bird," had waited so long for her to fledge that the result was both inevitable and predictable: I would be the one left behind. When Hannah took her maiden solo flight, it set off a chain reaction from my head to my heart. An endless cascade of emotions followed. I had imagined our separating differently.

We would, I thought, transition together seamlessly into a new adult relationship, a friendship. But instead, it was rather messy in the same way Reverend Jim always warned us from the pulpit: "Life is messy."

Hannah made a break for it after one particularly unpleasant phone conversation ended with me saying, "Let's stop here before we say anything we might regret."

I had been fully engaged in my mothering role. Again. She must have sensed some desperation in me to be done with the whole bloody mess. She, too, must have felt the time had come.

My afterthought to her was only: "I am sorry we argued."

She texted back the same. A month since our messy break-up, she is not ready to talk. She is sorting out things, she says in a text . . . does not want to hurt my feelings. My apology for having hurt hers fell into the cyberspace of unanswered messages.

I watch my phone more diligently for a call from her. I check the mail daily, thinking she might write out her thoughts rather than open up another confrontational conversation. My heart feels fragile. Her heart must, too. Her always sensitive self, no doubt, senses this monumental moment of having truly left the nest. If

I had been more sensitive myself, I might have stopped she pushing her off that ledge. If I had waited silently, rather than ver- bally forcing something to happen, we might both have felt better about the break.

I am left to wonder whether she would have willingly in her own time, like that last falcon chick, made the leap on her own. I wonder, too, whether that mother bird returned with food, as usual, only to find that her last baby had flown. Did the webcam capture that moment of love and loss? I wonder.

PART FOUR

The Pilgrimage

In Memory

"She embarked on the journey with deep intention . . . She pre-
pared like a pilgrim. She prayed, she created a ritual departure
beforehand by celebrating with friends and family, and she read
prodigiously, so that when she arrived at the different sites along
the pilgrimage she could exult in the 'thrill of recognition'. . . the
word thrill originally referred to the vibrations the arrow made
when it hits the target."[1]

The sea change in my heart began a year ago with a first and failed
attempt to make a pilgrimage. Alone on the screened lanai at midnight, under a waning summer moon that sits face to face with me
above the branch of my "sacred" tree, I share what I have yet to tell
anyone about my now-completed pilgrimage. I have come to see
that pilgrimages are private affairs.

Flickering moments come into view without warning. How
can I describe it? How do I speak about the sound of the long
"SSSSSSSSSSS" of the "SanctuSSSSS" sung at the Ely Cathedral
Lady's Chapel? Or the first early morning sight of a family of sev-
en swans gliding by on the river? Or the piercing screech of the

1. Cousineau, *The Art of Pilgrimage*, 182.

peregrines flying around the spire of Norwich Cathedral—and this just days after I watched them on my computer via webcam in Florida? Or the soft red glow from a candle I lit standing alone at the altar in Julian's anchorage? Or the airport terminals and train stations, where at all hours I waited in anticipation, all alone in a crowd? Or happening upon a little garden cafe in time for afternoon "tea and cakes," following a long day in the library? Or that unforgettable man on the plane fighting back tears while saying, "I am coming back from my grandson's funeral. He was climbing the Matterhorn and fell."

Wonder and weariness are part of anyone's pilgrimage. But the story is like a secret shared between the pilgrim and the sacred. This is the "pearl of great price," the boon, the gold. A gift so precious and so invaluable requires something of the pilgrim in return. It matters that I made this pilgrimage and that I have returned. Therefore, I think, the story must be told. So, here I sit with a pocketful of memories, wondering where and how to begin.

It all began with a long good-bye at Orlando International Airport, where Arthur and I shared a meal before we boarded separate flights. I would be going east across the Atlantic to Norwich, England, while he would go west across the U.S. to Seattle, Washington. We figured there was a ten-hour time difference between the two cities. When Arthur's flight was delayed, we had already said good-bye. So, we meandered together back and forth between our respective gates, a "couple of a certain age," full of youthful excitement.

We watched the overhead monitors for two flights and listened to broadcasts blaring through the terminals. At last, at 7 p.m. Eastern Standard Time, we heard boarding calls for our separate outgoing flights. Waving back and forth until we disappeared in the sea of people, we went our separate ways. One last text message between us from our seats on board, then the phones were turned off for the next two weeks.

The following morning, I found Gatwick International just as quiet as the Orlando airport was noisy. No loudspeaker announcements throughout the airport, no TVs, and no Muzak. Only the murmur of low voices of travelers watching monitors, waiting for gates to be posted.

"How civilized," I thought, walking the long hallways, following signs to the train station.

My plane had flown over the bright, sunny southeast coast of England, across miles of verdant green farmland after passing the unmistakable rugged White Cliffs of Dover on June 21, 2019, the first day of summer.

"Lovely," as the Brits say.

Later that morning, my arrival by train in London came as a jolt to my sleep-deprived senses. Thrust out into the busyness of rush hour, I wandered aimlessly in this direction then that, thinking surely the British Library would be right around the next corner. "Never mind," I thought, as I sat down at a sidewalk cafe to order breakfast.

The day was cool and breezy. I pulled a scarf from my suitcase. Consulting my GPS map, I decided to find my hotel, dump my luggage, then head for the library. By 3 p.m., I was a card-carrying member of the British Library, often referred to here as the BL.

"No pens allowed if you are going into the manuscripts room. You must leave your coat and bags in the lockers," said the clerk.

I recalled someone had warned me: "Don't forget your pencil." Now I knew why. Yet, I did not have a pencil in my backpack.

The low light matched the quiet of the second-floor study room. I presented my new photo ID. Three manuscripts I had ordered online from home were waiting for me. From the tall oak bookcase with leaded glass doors, an equally tall librarian took two books and a box from the shelf.

"These can be photographed, so please sit in that section," he said, placing them into my open hands, ready to receive.

I thought, "He's just going to give these to me?"

The largest book with a powder-blue cover was imprinted with a gold insignia. I opened it first, carefully perching it on the pillowed stand. Slanted handwriting in Middle English filled the facing pages of the oversized book. The smaller book's binding read "*British Museum Sloane 2499.*" I wondered why the library would have it in their collection. The first page was in bold Medieval typeface:

XVI Revelations of Divine Love shewed to a devout servant of our Lord, called Mother Juliana, an anchorine of Norwich who lived in the days of King Henry the Third.[2]

I got goosebumps.

"I made it," thought I, feeling my happiest smile.

The year's wait made it seem all the sweeter. Savoring the moment, I slowly opened a pastel blue-green box. When I gingerly lifted the flaps from the cover, I felt like a ten-year-old on Christmas morning. I knew what was in that box. It was the second of the Sloane manuscripts, which had been copied from the first. Some scholars say this version has many "eye skips," lines "skipped" by the scribes. I could not tell the difference. To my eyes, Middle English looks like beautiful calligraphy. Practically speaking, it is almost unreadable. Nonetheless, I sat surrounded by this old, perfectly maintained collection of Julian of Norwich's profound thoughts, handwritten hundreds of years earlier. When I asked the librarian why it was stamped "British Museum," he seemed to relish in sharing his story:

"The British Museum was the library before this building was built in the 1970s. I worked there when the collection was moved over from there to here," he said with a wistful look.

Beside him, his much younger, wide-eyed coworker listened intently to his story. She added that it had taken twenty years to build this new British Library.

"Everything you see here was once in the British Museum, and that is why things from the archive are stamped with this red insignia," he said, holding up the book to examine it. "These are in really good shape," he added more or less to himself.

Julian's original writing went underground for many years. These copies of Julian's text did not surface during her lifetime because people were being persecuted by the Roman Catholic Church for writing far less. The content itself would have been reason enough to keep it secret, but the fact that it was written in English was enough to get one killed. So-called heretics, commonly known around Norwich as "Lollards," were being killed for possessing

2. Cressy, *XVI Revelations,* Sloane Ms. 2499.

Bibles translated into English. The church's language was Latin. During those Dark Ages, men, women, and children were burned and dumped at "Lollards Pit," not far from Julian's anchorage. My apartment while in Norwich on pilgrimage was on Lollard's Road!

It was a small group of women who fled England to begin a convent in Cambrai, France who most likely carried Julian's text with them among their belongings. While they lived in exile during days when monasteries and convents were being dissolved by King Henry VIII, these Sisters painstakingly hand-wrote several copies of Julian's original work, perhaps as many as seven copies existed at one time.

Before arriving in England, I had requested to see all the manuscripts that I knew to be available in England. Neither Norwich Castle nor Westminster Abbey could accommodate me. The three copies, which I had before me, served my purposes, having already listened to an audio version of the full text as preparation for my pilgrimage. Comparing my own notes with the handwritten manuscript, I was able to search out Julian's oft-quoted words, as translated from Middle English: *"All shall be well. And all shall be most well. And all manner of things shall be well."*[3]

I took a photograph, then immediately sent it via email to all those special ones back home, or as Julian would have said, "all my even-Christians." Responses came quickly, despite the time difference.

"I am so glad you are there," said one.

"Wow. I can read the words." said another.

These friends had now joined me on my solo pilgrimage.

The BL was a lovely place for a pilgrim to spend her first day. I stayed until closing and planned to return first thing the next morning. In between, the clock seemed to stop in real time, allowing for a moment of serendipity my first Saturday on the streets of London.

After breakfast in my boutique hotel, I walked in the direction of the BL. My head would have been in the clouds, except for the red double-decker buses squeezing so closely to the sidewalk. I had to watch my toes. I made a spur-of-the-moment decision to go to

---

3. Cressy, *XVI Revelations*, Sloane Ms. 2499.

the train station to pick up my ticket to Norwich on my way to the BL. Ticket in hand, I exited the massive station on the opposite side from the library without realizing that I could have simply walked across the street to the BL. Instead, I walked down Euston Street. Waiting patiently for the pedestrian signal at a very busy intersection, I overheard two British women standing beside me discussing directions.

"Nobody asks for directions here in London," said one.

"It is around the British Library," replied the other.

Turning my face toward them, I said, "If it helps, the British Library is just in the next block on the right."

"Well, we are not actually going to the library, we are looking for the Quaker Friends Meetinghouse," said the older one, who appeared to be about my age.

"Really?" I said with surprise.

"Are you a Friend?" she asked.

With that one simple exchange, an amazing chain reaction began.

Now a Pilgrim

The two women jested about being "country bumpkins" in London for an interfaith day at the Quaker Friends Meetinghouse. When one asked if I was a "Friend," she had no idea we were about to become fast friends. We carried our conversation across the chaotic intersection without skipping a beat.

"If I did not have a noon train to catch to Norwich, I would love to join you," I said, wishing I could be in two places at once.

"Going to Nor'ich?" one of them replied in a sing-song voice.

"Yes, I am going to see Julian of Norwich's anchorage."

She stopped walking, leaned backward and burst out, "Really? We were just talking about Julian!"

"You were?" I asked, stopping too.

Suddenly, we were laughing like three schoolgirls, walking down Euston on a leisurely Saturday morning. Then, all too soon, we waved goodbye, as I peeled off in the direction of the library.

The black iron gates were closed, so I stepped up to see the posted hours. It would be thirty minutes before I could enter.

My first thought was: "I have time for a cappuccino," as I looked toward a sidewalk cafe, I noticed the day before.

Instead, I turned in the direction where those women were headed.

When I caught up with them, I said, "I would like to go with you."

The older one, whose name was Marjorie, said she knew little about the day's agenda, except that the first thing was a charismatic Mass.

"There it is," she said, pointing across the street to a red brick building with a flag that said "Friends."

The younger woman, Araminta, offered to buy me a cup of tea. We found a table inside the Friends' cafe and got right to the heart of things: Marjorie had been a life-long Catholic, while Araminta claimed no faith tradition.

"What I admire about Marjorie is how she wears her faith on her sleeve," said Araminta.

Looking at Marjorie, I said, "How un-British of you."

We laughed, as I continued. "I was the youth-group coordinator years ago at the Cambridge Friends Meetinghouse in Massachusetts. We made an interfaith pilgrimage through the city by attending services each week at a different church, mosque, temple, or synagogue. These days, I organize lifelong learners to help them write spiritual autobiographies."

Araminta raised her hand to her heart. "I want to write my story. I had no faith upbringing, but I have had some amazing experiences that changed my life."

Marjorie explained that her church and others in her village were organizing themselves to engage as one interfaith community.

"They would love to have you come to lead a spiritual autobiography. I have a big house. Lots of bedrooms," she said, while removing a tea bag from her paper cup.

"What are we supposed to do with this and tea in paper cups?" she asked of her friend with disgust.

"It's the American way," I said sheepishly.

"I see," Marjorie said in that upper-crust tone the Brits have perfected.

The room was filling up, and we knew we had little time to waste. We quickly wrote our email addresses on brown paper napkins before joining a bustling crowd making its way into the building.

Quakers are silent worshipers. Nonetheless, this interfaith day opened with a charismatic rock-music Mass. We were given wristbands that said: *"You will receive power."* I had wanted to step inside the meetinghouse to see their worship space, but the music went on for fifteen minutes or so. With hugs from my new friends, I left.

Crossing the street, I entered the quiet hum of the British Library, a great contrast to the ruckus of that first early morning.

When I was sitting once again with three hand-copied manuscripts, I noticed my new rubber wristband, *"You will receive power."* Was this to be my pilgrimage message? A touchstone? I decided I would wear it for the duration, as a reminder of the serendipity with strangers in London. Today, it is part of what I call my "collectibles," which I see every day on my writing table.

I love to play back this uncanny episode in my mind. Early that morning, when those two women arrived by train, I was in the same station buying my ticket. We must have exited at about the same moment to wind up standing side by side on the corner. How often serendipity has played out like this in my life, I cannot say, but I believe it happens more often than I know.

"In sacred travel, every experience is uncanny. No encounter is without meaning. There are signs everywhere, . . ."[1]

Moments like these defy explanation. But clearly, they are meant to be, as if divinely ordered. The further away I am from that day in London, the clearer I see those two women in my mind's eye. But, mostly, I hear our laughter, like that of carefree children just released from class. Once we met, I was released from my normal life. I was suddenly and consciously a true pilgrim.

1. Cousineau, *The Art of Pilgrimage*, 97.

Norwich

(sounds like porridge)

June 22, 2019

For months I had pictured Norwich as a small village with cottages, cows, sheep, and a small church with an anchorage, plus one great big Cathedral. Well, I was right about one thing, the Cathedral. It is undeniable.

The soaring spire reaches skyward, 315 feet, and is the second tallest in all of England. A medieval rose-draped stone wall forms a "close" around Norwich Cathedral. The footpaths are statued with ancient trees standing as tall as they are wide. Most days, I followed a footpath under a canopy that seemed like a sprawling, cedar-scented outdoor Cathedral. I wondered whether one old tree predated the Cathedral, which was completed around the twelfth century.

A river-walk historical marker at Pull's Ferry says barges carried stones from Caen in Normandy, France, up the River Wensum and then via a canal built by the monks so the massive Cathedral could be constructed. Today, canal boats and swans, as picturesque as can be, make it hard to imagine those barges moving along this waterway weighted down with heavy stones.

Once I got settled in my apartment, I began writing an "evening missive" to send home via email. These reflections from a wandering pilgrim helped preserve moment-to-moment experiences:

It is 10 p.m. and still completely light outside. The sun rose around 5:30 in London, as did I. But now I am in Norwich, further east . . . at long last. It's the summer solstice.

I went on a wander and found the Cathedral. Not too difficult because of its soaring spire. It is almost directly across the river from my house. At 6 p.m. the gatekeeper was locking up, but I managed to slip inside for a few minutes. Gorgeous. Tomorrow, I plan to attend evensong and walk the labyrinth.

When I saw the peregrines, I nearly cried to see all three of them. I intend to talk with those who have been watching them with telescopes from the ground. I can hardly wait to say, "I've watched them from Florida." How super cool is that? The village is larger than I expected but oozing with charm. I will find Julian tomorrow and report back.

P.S.: The two women I told you about knew without my saying so that I was on a pilgrimage.

Touch of Home

After three days of reading and writing in the Norwich Cathedral library, the librarian asked: "Are you staying in Norwich?"

I said I was there to do research on Julian. I did not call it a pilgrimage.

I asked her about some of the many authors whose books I was reading. Had they come to the library to do their research?

"Some are well-known figures around here," she said.

"Are you writing a book?" she asked.

All legitimate questions, I suppose. I had not come with the intention of writing a book, I was on a pilgrimage. But I did not say, "I am a pilgrim," despite months of preparation. I still felt uncomfortable saying those words out loud here.

Instead, I asked the librarian whether she sometimes went across town to the anchorage?

"Sometimes, when I want a quiet place alone, I go to sit there," she said.

I wanted to say I was on a pilgrimage to do that same thing, but I didn't.

"There seems to be more interest from Americans in Julian these days," she added.

I prepared a cup of tea from the library's bottomless kettle and took a seat by the window. I caught glimpses of the peregrines overhead, soaring and screeching. It could not have been more perfect.

The Cathedral is a very active place. In fact, from Sunday morning until evensong each day throughout the week, people were everywhere. Some were tourists, but not all. Students from the

Norwich Cathedral School, located on the grounds, were unmistakable in their blue-and-green uniforms. Their sweet voices sang services within the Cathedral each day and during special celebrations. The refectory served breakfast and lunch to people from all walks of life from everywhere. I heard German, French, and Spanish spoken as I sipped my morning cappuccino. Norwich has had close ties over the years with the Netherlands and Northern Europe.

The cloister, a covered walkway encircling the courtyard, would have at one time been the pathway for monks to get from one end of the Cathedral to the other, perhaps in silence. Today, the relentless foot traffic reminds me of Grand Central Station during rush hour. Sometimes people would eat their lunch on the steps, looking up at the peregrine falcons. There is a labyrinth at the center of the courtyard. One day I saw students in Shakespearean costumes practicing a play.

"The church is alive here," I thought. It was such a contrast to some mostly deserted churches I've seen in so many places. The voluminous and magnificent sanctuary, the courtyard labyrinth, and the pealing bells called people together. Those who did not care to enter for prayer, gathered outside to enjoy the peregrines, circling and screeching—screeching, screeching—all day long. Heads were continually lifted upward. I certainly felt uplifted.

I spoke frequently to Hawk and Owl Trust volunteers who kept telescopes trained on the peregrines. They seemed excited to be reminded that the webcam they positioned on the man-made nesting platform high up on the Cathedral was exposing the birds to the wide, wide world.

Perhaps they thought I was an intrepid globe-trotting bird watcher, rather than a pilgrim. I did not tell these aviary scientists that I was at least equally interested in Julian's enclosed life. The three fledgling falcons, flying freely to and fro, were in training. Their parents lured them further and further away from the nest with food, providing less and less over time, until each learned to hunt on its own. When the fledglings finally fly away, leaving their parents behind for good, the webcam goes dark until the following spring. The parents will stay put for another nesting season. Peregrine falcons mate for life. I knew I would be watching them again ſne following year, but I had not the tiniest inkling that I would be in quarantine during a global pandemic that would for me shed some light on the plague which afflicted Norwich in the Middle Ages. Clearly, I had come to Norwich at the auspicious time.

One day, I noticed a sign posted at the door to the library: "World Community for Christian Meditation, Tuesday, 13:00, St. Catherine's Chapel." This was Tuesday. I asked the librarian to point me in the right direction.

She leaped out of her swirling chair and walked with me down the stairs.

"Just walk through the cloister to that far-right door," she said pointing in that direction.

I did as she instructed. Inside the massive Cathedral, I did not see at first glance which side chapel might be the one. I asked a man with a duster in hand, cleaning the altar, if he might know. Yes, he knew exactly where I wanted to go. The glass door was painted with pink angels and three sparkly words: "St. Catherine's Chapel." Inside the round room, high windows let in early afternoon sunlight, and three women were seated on a curved bench. I took a seat at the end.

"Welcome. Are you here for meditation?" one of them asked.

"Yes, I am."

"Have you meditated before?" another asked.

"Yes, at home I also meditate on Tuesdays with a small group from the World Community for Christian Meditation," I said.

We smiled at one another. The gong sounded. A poem was read aloud. I said my mantra. It was all so familiar. With eyes closed, I could not tell the difference between here and home. This thirty minutes in silence with strangers was a lovely touch of home. I never felt at all homesick in Norwich.

Immediately afterward, someone asked, "How long will you be in Norwich?"

"I am on a pilgrimage to the anchorage," I said unequivocally for the first time.

This marked a turning point in my pilgrimage. I had completely crossed over the threshold. My destination had been reached, but the return was not yet on the horizon. I was still in a state of astonishment, a liminal, in-between place, on the pilgrimage. No pilgrimage is complete without entering this space. It is never certain when or where this might happen. It is not something that can be planned. I sent a message home to tell my meditation group that I had joined them that very day from Norwich. Here are some other thoughts from my evening missive:

I am officially living on British Summer Time, i.e., drinking afternoon "tea and cakes" and eating late-evening meals. It is a change; my internal clock is somewhere between England and America.

Someone said to me: "I detect a slight North American accent." Slight, I doubt, compared to these beautifully, soothing accents all around.

If we think the church is dead, it is not so here, or at least at the Cathedral. The place is abuzz all day with activities.

Admiring the falcons took up much of my attention, as they are still flying around the spire and screeching overhead and soaring with prey. The Hawk and Owl Trust is in residence with telescopes, and they will talk as long as you want. I wanted to, and learned so, so much. I bought a photo taken of the falcon first to fledge this year. I will put it somewhere so I can see it every day when I get back home. When the three fledglings flew right over me as I walked the labyrinth, I took that as some sort of sign. All three peregrines survived their pilgrimage flight.

The Bishopsgate Garden was open today, one of only three times all year! Such a lovely walled joy of scents and colors. I roamed the many mazes in between daisies, roses, foxgloves. Colors and scents linger.

The evensong was a special musical event with the Bishop presiding, staff in hand. The festival chorus was made up of one hundred voices from choirs of Norwich and from other parts of Norfolk county, the easternmost of English counties. They sang, we sang, and the pipe organ bellowed out everything from a march to a subtle, nearly a cappella, sound. Wowzer!

I am amazed at how efficient my digs are from the shower to the stove. This is a fourteenth-century world meeting twenty-first century needs. Why don't we North Americans do this better?

Now that I am more or less familiar with this loveliest of walking villages and its flowered, ancient walls, I know how I'm going to spend my next few days.

Tomorrow is Julian's Day. I hope I can sleep tonight. I want to attend the morning Mass celebrated in her anchorage!

The Interior World of an Anchoress

Sitting alone in Mother Julian's anchorage, I tried to imagine what it might feel like to live in such a place until my last breath. The wooden double doors here would have been nailed shut in Julian's time. There would have been no electricity. The stained-glass windows can let in some natural light, but the candlelight and outside light, combined, did not brighten this studio-size space. I couldn't believe I was here, at long last, all alone in the anchorage.

Hearing two young men outside in the garden, chatting and smoking cigarettes, reminded me once again that the anchoress was in a state of exile. Other people exist out there.

Staring me in the face was Julian's altar, engraved with the words: *"Thou art enough for me."* The crucifix above was the only reference point. I knew she meant what she said by her actions. She lived out her life in this space, alone with Christ, day and night. I did not doubt her motives or sincerity.

The longer I sat, the more uncomfortable I became. Not only did the dampness and coolness seep into my bones, but a sense of insignificance was permeating my mind.

"I am a mere speck in the universe," I realized in a way I had not thought about before. I felt as insignificant as the dust I would one day become. Mortality, with a capital "M," seemed to be in the room with me. My mortality.

Before coming here, I thought I could be an anchoress, living in self-imposed exile from the wider world. But the truth, my truth, became clear in that room.

I know in my heart that my soul is my essence, but my head spoke up in contradiction: "I could not do this," I said to the walls, to the crucifix, to Julian, to God, to myself.

"At least there is an exit," I thought, eyeing the door which was not there for Julian. Her place of exile was fixed and known to everyone in her world. Anchoresses stay put; pilgrims are free to go. I felt it a great relief to be a pilgrim, free to get up and walk out of that cell. I left after one hour.

I did not experience a feeling of claustrophobia such as my daughter once had when we entered the Mammoth Caves in Kentucky. Nor did I feel a fear of living as a solitary, without someone to share my life. Or a feeling of loneliness, which no doubt would have crept into the anchorage. No, it was Tolstoy's abyss that presented itself: Those depths so "unfathomable" as to be "unimaginable." That was what I felt in the dimming afternoon light, sitting all alone, staring at those words carved in stone in the altar: *Thou art enough for me.* I mentioned my private experience within the anchorage to the priest and Julian Center librarian.

"It's not for everybody," was his response. True enough. It was surely not for me. I was relieved to know what I could not have known before spending time alone within those anchorage walls.

Women for ages have sought a "room of our own." And this has become more attainable for women in this century than it was in the Middle Ages. For Julian, it must have been the ultimate experience, foreclosing all else, except writing, praying, and offering spiritual direction. For me, my so-called anchorage in Florida feels more like an "in-betweenness," a borderland, "of" but, not "in" a world that is always calling. The depth of an interior life often is measured by a person's ability to withdraw from the world at large. Contemplatives require a quiet and solitary world. I, too, love this quieter aspect of my "third life." In many ways, it is a novelty after a lifetime of motherhood.

This novelty, this birthing of a new "being," has been difficult, like any birth. It has required a lot of painful pushing and pulling, letting go, surrendering what once was for what is apparently meant to be. Each step of separation from my daughter this past year has felt like separating from my all-encompassing motherly role.

These painful birthing moments of mother and daughter emerging as new individuals create angst and relief for both of us, a mutual laboring, then resting. The pangs of separation remain palpable. But like childbirth, the memories lessen over time.

This process of change seems so s-l-o-w, "slow as molasses," my mother might have said. I recall vividly that she would disappear into the one-and-only bathroom in our tiny ranch house. It was her makeshift anchorage. Likewise, I often retreated to my backyard garden during years of motherhood. It was a sort of anchorage in some ways. That earthy, exterior world seemed to open up my interior world.

The low fence surrounding the garden was a gentle boundary against the outside domestic world. The weeds I pulled drew me deeper into a contemplative place hour after hour. I felt invisibly visible under my wide-brimmed hat. Everyone knew where I could be found, but they hardly noticed me there. I was a familiar figure in my garden, like Lady Julian under her veil in her more permanent anchorage.

That garden is gone from my present life, along with my young children. Now, different hats cover my head from the harsh tropical sun at my new home in Florida, where I grow herbs in pots on the screened lanai.

Just beyond the lanai is the river, where abundant wildlife maneuver about from dawn to dusk. My "one and only" Afrika tree is a steady reminder to "be still" and to breathe. I feel connected to the whole of life there, even as I sometimes choose to step back from life in the outside social world.

Sleepless

June 26, 2019

At the midpoint of the pilgrimage, I could not sleep. My nightly pattern had shifted to staying awake so much later than at home. Hannah texted from her late-night gallery work: "Can't sleep again?" It was not the only shift happening.

I could not be sure when it began, but my emotions had settled. For so many years I had prayed these words: "Your will, not mine," while in my heart I was holding on to some thread of what I wanted for fear of letting go. Somehow, the letting go had happened. This was not a conscious act.

In the morning, I made my way to the train bound for Ely Cathedral and a noon concert. This day, an a cappella chorus from Sweden performed in the Lady's Chapel, a stark room with only one statue of a woman robed in blue aloft at the front of the room.

The soft voices in the chorale reverberated around us. When the singers lined up on the walls around us, it was live surround-sound. The first "S" of the Sanctus was echoed from the first singer until the last sang that whispered "Ssss." Their final note hung in the air. It was the balm I needed on my pilgrimage. Music has always come to the rescue when I needed it most.

Outside that chapel, the museum-like Cathedral was dark in contrast with Norwich's, except for candles burning at various altars. I approached one, picked up a match, and lit a glass votive candle. I said silently: "For my heart to heal." Beside the candles, I noticed some small cards with a photo of the woman's statue in the Lady's Chapel. I tucked it into my pocket.

The weather was raw and gray with a stiff wind off the water where boats were bobbing on their moorings reminding me of Cape Cod. "I should have worn my heavy raincoat," I thought as I waited for the train with workers who had begun gathering on the platform. Two men in bright orange overalls took their seats behind me in the car. They talked loudly and incessantly as we moved from one small village station to the next. I wanted to bask in the music that was still ringing in my head, but could not.

I heard someone say to them, "Did you mean to go all the way to Norwich?" Suddenly, they realized they had missed their stop. They disembarked at the next station. Peace at last. I reached into my pocket and felt the little card in my hand. It read:

> "For centuries people came to Ely as pilgrims to visit the shrine of Etheldreda, who founded the monastery here in 673 AD. They came to give thanks, to pray for healing, to ask for forgiveness, to seek God's guidance. What is it that you are seeking from God?"

Directly below was a reply:

> "I am seeking. I am hesitant and uncertain, but will you, O God, watch over each step of mine and guide me in your way. Amen. A prayer of St. Augustine."

A prayer meant for me, a pilgrim from St. Augustine? I pondered that thought all the way back to Norwich. Once inside my "home away from home," I saw an email from Arthur: "Back home, safe and sound."

Thou Art Enough for Me

As a pilgrim, I was learning how exile draws one deeper into oneself as it draws one away from all the old familiar places. A universal yearning, a quest, especially from the brokenheartedness of life, calls to us from a very deep place. By isolating oneself for a time, one sees that those who may be part of our story do not own it. Be it mother, father, child, friend, or lover, they are not the keepers of the story. At most they are witnesses to the truth of one's story.

They were there. They saw things with their own eyes. They have their own versions of the day we met, the night we cried, and the times we laughed. Witnesses are valuable truth-tellers in so far as what they know. If they were present for moments that mattered, all the better. More often than not, the truth appears in solitary moments. Truth with a big "T" does not require witnesses to attest to any of the facts. That Truth belongs only to oneself. It is what one eventually learns to live by and to trust at all times. Discovering one's own truth, takes time, perhaps a lifetime.

The truth of my solo pilgrimage, embedded within my self-imposed exile, is that there were no witnesses. That truth found me when I was alone in Julian's anchorage. The years came together there through private tears. I was alone—all alone in the world— just as when I was a child and my cartoon friend, Mr. Magoo, sang to me: *"I'm all alone in the world."*

This aloneness, after six decades, penetrated my heart's inner chamber within Julian's holy chamber. For all the years and people filling up my life, the truth is: I am alone; not unloved nor unattached, but alone, nonetheless. That truth has no witness other than the "One." To discover this truth is to know it for all time. I had come a long way to rediscover what I had once known as a young girl alone in my favorite tree.

For a long while that day in Norwich, I sat with only the crucifix and Julian's altar looking back at me. Inscribed in the marble before me were her own words: *"Thou art enough for me."* I knew she was head over heels in love by those simple, but powerfully sobering words, *"Thou art enough for me."* I was humbled, sitting silently before those words. Julian had written:

> *"Our Lord God also showed that it gives him very great pleasure when a simple soul comes to him in a bare, plain and familiar way. For, as I understand this showing, it is the natural yearning of the soul touched by the Holy Ghost to say, 'God, of your goodness, give me yourself; you are enough for me'"* . . .[1]

The words began to nag at me. After my self-imposed exile and after making my long-awaited pilgrimage, truth is, I could not say these same words. I need others in my life. I love them. I would miss them as sorely as I miss all those who have disappeared one way or another from my life. This solitary life of an anchoress would not be "enough" for me. It made me sad to see the truth. My heart was melting, melting, melting like the candles on the stone-cold marble altar with its inscription speaking across centuries.

The two red votive candles I lit flickered in the late afternoon sunlight streaming through the stained glass. I felt chilly and pulled a scarf from my backpack. I wanted and needed to understand why in the world I was sitting there all alone this Friday afternoon in late June. Why had I come all this way? To be alone? To feel this poignant aloneness in the vast universe? Had that call to pilgrimage actually been a "siren's call" that mocked me? Was it not obvious in the twenty-first century, living as I do in Florida, that I would never become an anchoress? What was I taking home with me from this pilgrimage across the ocean? A few hazelnuts to give away to friends? I was dismayed by the truth. I began to gather my things to leave. I heard people entering the church for an evening service

1. Spearing, *Revelations of Divine Love*, 48.

I had planned to attend. There was only one way out. It was not possible for me to slip away.

As a consequence, I was there in the anchorage with others when my prayer "For my heart to heal" was read aloud that evening at Mass. I had written it on the first day of my pilgrimage.

However, when a young, bespectacled, priest spoke my prayer out loud, he said, "For *their* hearts to heal." Not only my heart, but another's heart along with mine was being offered up. Those words resonated so deeply that I could not stop thinking about it during the rest of the service, which proceeded with rote words and rituals I knew by heart. Never before had I felt the impact of my own prayer quite this way.

I had left this same prayer "for my heart to heal" upon many other altars during my pilgrimage. It was a prayer made straight from my heart, for my heart. Yet it was more than that. It had become, in the context of my pilgrimage and exile, the answer to what I had been seeking for such a long, long time. Now it was clear that it was the right request in the right place at the right time. I knew this was the truth because I felt so much lighter as I walked away from the anchorage for the last time. I said goodbye to Julian and to those with whom I had prayed. As I walked along the now-familiar route from the anchorage to my riverside apartment, I was aware that my pilgrimage was not yet over, but my heart knew I had already changed.

Ready, Set . . .

June 30, 2019

The return begins when thoughts turn toward leaving. A warm early morning greeting matched the day. Araminta wrote in a hasty email to me:

"You have probably already left, but I wanted to say goodbye. I so loved our tea at the Friends in London."

Facing a two-day journey, I assessed my baggage. I had not bought anything that would add weight to my suitcases. I had come with more clothes than I needed, per usual. In particular, I had a long raincoat, because the week before my departure, England had been deluged by cold torrential rains. So much so that the National Rail had cancelled trains due to flooding.

The temperatures had not moved much toward summer during my pilgrimage. Based on a friend's advice, I had packed my practical, waterproof, black coat instead of my light and impractical stylish leather jacket. For the entire week, after carrying the raincoat through airports, train stations, and the Underground, the coat stayed over the back of a chair in the apartment. I preferred to layer sweaters against the coolness and wrap a scarf around my neck rather than wear that coat. It did not rain once.

This last morning, recalling the many times I had walked past a thrift shop at St. Martin's homeless shelter, I picked up that raincoat, threw it over my arm, and headed across the river's footbridge for the final time. The coat was perfect for the raw coastal climates of Norwich and Cape Cod, where I lived when I bought it. I knew that someone living in Norwich would get a lot more use from it than I ever would again in sunny, warm Florida. It felt right to leave it at the donation door. And once again, I felt lighter.

The day of departure, June 30, seemed to be the most beautiful summer morning I could ever remember. There was just enough time for another riverside walk to see the swans with their young'uns and more importantly, to watch the peregrines overhead one last time before my noon train.

I found a bench under a sprawling tree, which was the perfect perch for watching weekend pleasure boaters. On the opposite bank, a mother duck basked with her brood in the sun. The breezes felt mild on my face. The Cathedral bells chimed the quarter hours. I was reluctant to move from this spot. The words "River Friends" were carved into the bench. I recalled my first day in the UK and the two new friends I had made in London who knew immediately that I was a pilgrim. I thought about my group of "River Writers" back home and our gatherings on the river porch. I had put away four hazelnuts in my backpack, one for each of them.

I lingered leisurely, preparing interiorly for my return. All pilgrims must return home for the pilgrimage to be complete. I would have to let the peregrines grow up on their own.

Back at the apartment, I packed a photo of the first fledgling among other treasures, then locked the door for the final time. I walked the now-familiar street to the train station, wheeling my suitcase behind me. I arrived too early for my scheduled ticket.

The train official said, "Just put your feet up," when I asked about boarding an earlier train, so I sat in the pub. Did I hear one of the blokes say something about the Boston Red Sox? Suddenly, I longed for home. My brother would tell me later: "I looked for you on TV during the Red Sox game in London."

The first stop on my pilgrimage return was London. I reluctantly reentered the world of Saturday shoppers, families, friends, and lovers. Retracing my steps to the British Library, I recalled my first day of this nearly completed pilgrimage. I did not need to see Julian's manuscripts again, but I loved being in the library. Today it felt like seeing an old friend. In the gift shop, I bought my daughter

DY, SET . . .

a present for her twenty-ninth birthday, just days away. I sent an email to tell her so.

"Let me guess. Another book?" she replied, signaling mild distress from across the ocean. It brought to mind my return from Morocco when she was a twelve-year-old. I phoned when I got to New York to say, "I am back in the country."

"Is it Okay if I sleep over at Emily's?" she asked.

I let it go both times. The return was calling, and "*Thou art enough for me*" was still running through my mind.

The next morning, an outbound flight to Canada took me back over the English countryside. In typical fashion, I put in my earphones to block out my surroundings. I had the whole seven-hour trip planned in my mind. The remaining, still-empty journal that I had saved for this moment was on my tray table before me. As everyone settled into seats, I noticed a young couple across from me talking to one another. She was in the seat behind him. I remembered times when others had given up their seats so I could sit with my traveling partner. I considered offering my seat to the young woman while assessing the situation. She was in the middle section of the plane in a row of three. I was on the aisle beside an older man who had simply nodded to me when I sat down. It was going to be a long flight. I did not offer to change seats.

As we taxied away, I said in my heart: "Goodbye England and all things English."

We flew back over the countryside, but clouds obscured it from view. Out of sight, out of mind? I began to write in my journal:

"I have seven hours above the world in which to write uninterrupted thoughts. Where to begin? First, I did it! Every last detail worked out. Second, the unexpected happened in a chance meeting with two women who led me to the Quaker Friends that first morning. Third, all three peregrine fledglings and both parents circled the Norwich Cathedral every single day. That Cathedral defies description, but when music bellows through its organ pipes and those young choristers sing, not even a choir of angels could be more lovely.

Silent candles burn on side altars around the voluminous sanctuary. The "peace globe" candelabra is unlike anything I have seen in any Cathedral, including Notre Dame in Paris. There my daughter lit a candle for me, as I had once lit a candle for my mother. In Norwich, I lit one for each of them. This is what Julian is all about: mothering love guaranteed unconditionally, endlessly, and eternally.

One thing I learned on my journey is that Julian's actual anchorage did not survive the Reformation period and that St. Julian's Church was all but destroyed in World War II. Both, however, were rebuilt over time and then reopened serendipitously the year of my birth. We, the buildings and I, turned the age of sixty-five together."

After a few hours, my ruminations were interrupted by the man seated beside me. When he returned from the bathroom, he spoke to me for the first time.

"Are you a writer?" he asked.

"Yes, I am writing a book," I said.

"I thought so," he said, glancing at the open journal.

After sharing that I had been to Norwich, I asked quite innocently whether he was returning home.

"Yes, I went to England for my grandson's funeral," his voice choking on his words. "He was twenty-four years old. He was climbing the Matterhorn and fell," he added, turning to look out the window.

I put my pencil down and closed my journal. For several hours we talked, and the conversation kept coming back around to his grandson:

"He was always a daredevil. I took him up to the Space Needle in Toronto when he was ten," he said, tears filling his eyes. "He hung over the edge in the wind, laughing."

As I listened, I remembered how close I had come to giving up my seat to someone else. Would he have told that person his story? Maybe, but I believe I was meant to hear it. This was part of my pilgrimage return. When we finally landed in Toronto, I put my hand on his shoulder.

"I am really sorry," was all I could manage to say as we locked eyes.

"Go home and hug your grandkids," he replied.

Return

July 1, 2020

If you ever want to see an airport awaken for the day, show up pre-dawn. At 4:00 a.m. there were so few humans in the wide halls of Toronto's airport that it seemed unnatural. The security personnel were idly chatting, and the conveyor belts were empty of the usual clutter. Nobody seemed to notice the few early passengers going through the motions. Nonetheless, Muzak filled the emptiness, which felt as vast as some of the English cathedrals I'd been visiting. It was as far from a sacred space as any place on God's green earth. I was reminded once again of the "insignificance" I felt in Julian's anchorage.

An unexpected seat change made by Air Canada put me in first class. Oh Canada! I felt pride swell up from my own French-Canadian roots when the Captain said: "Happy Canada Day." I was going home via my grandparents' homeland. My grandfather, Arthur, and my grandmother, Marie Laure, my namesake, were born in Quebec City. They were immigrants to the United States with their burgeoning family. My mother was a first-generation American citizen. When I saw the small American flag over the entry doorway in Customs, my heart leaped a little. I was home.

"Yes, I am an American Citizen," I said, remembering Big Bend Border Patrol.

"I was on a pilgrimage in Norwich," I unabashedly told the border agent.

Crossing over any border or threshold is an important part of a pilgrimage. The return becomes a story within a story. The homeland calls the pilgrim back, much the same way the pilgrimage once beckoned.

Completing the pilgrimage brings emotional release. For every pilgrim the return is different, but significant no matter what. The young man who had died while climbing in Switzerland had left his home and reached his destination, but never returned.

The pilgrimage itself is an in-between place, a borderland, a place of exile from one's home. Julian perpetually lived between two worlds: church and village. She did not leave her homeland, yet she lived out her life in exile. She stayed put, and people have been going to Norwich to commune with her for centuries.

In her writings, Julian wonders why she should have been saved on her deathbed? Why should she, a "lowly creature," have been shown the visions of Christ? "Why me?" she wants to know. It took eighty-five chapters, written over some decades in exile, for Julian to explain this to herself and to the world.

When an unexplainable and mystical moment is bestowed, the accompanying, rhetorical "Why?" or "Why me, a lowly creature?" seems to follow naturally.

Since early childhood, I have had a sense of "being protected." It is not clear where or when that might have started, but I have lived my entire life with that innate knowing.

A week after the departure from Norwich, I sat at home at sunrise, feeling free of some things I had been carrying far too long. That raincoat I left behind, a black one, a heavy one, a lined one—all intended for protection against the elements of the world—was telling. My very own heart, I realized, had been clothed in some sort of protection during my time of exile.

I never assumed this protection to be something I was choosing to carry around, like my raincoat. Rather, I felt cloaked in this protection. It did not seem dark or heavy. It made me feel special, chosen or called. Why else should I have been protected throughout my lifelong pilgrimage on earth? Why me, "a lowly creature?"

Surely my choices and decisions over the years have not warranted it. At any moment, my entire life could have skidded off the rails. I had come dangerously close, yet I was always pulled back from going over the edge of the abyss. If I could attribute that rescuing hand to another person, I would. But there was no such person. Yet, I know in retrospect, beyond any doubt, that I was protected.

For weeks after returning home, Julian's phrase *"Thou art enough for me"* lingered in my thoughts. One day, out of the blue, I suddenly realized that those words were meant *for* me! Like seeing something in bold relief, I saw those words from a different perspective: *"Thou art enough for me"* no longer meant only that God was enough, it also meant that I am enough. Enough for God.

PART FIVE

Post Pilgrimage

Two Rivers

Here and There

July 20, 2019

In August 1953, I was pushed out into the world. My mother's memory after many decades was only that "it was a hot day." Indeed, late summer in rural New England is hot. That same year, the village of Norwich, England, celebrated another birth. That year the church of St. Julian was reopened after being bombed nearly to the ground during the Norwich blitz in 1942. The cell was destroyed at the Reformation, but because of the growing popularity of Julian's writings the church was rebuilt, and the original foundations of Julian's Cell were discovered, and a chapel built on the site.

Alongside this small parish church, the anchorage that had been in existence in the Middle Ages, came back to life, as did an attached cylindrical bell tower. Sixty-five years later, I can say from first-hand experience, that "all is well" at St. Julian's on Rouen Road, just across the River Wensum via the Lady Julian Bridge.

When I crossed that footbridge for the first time at 9 a.m. on Monday, June 24, 2019, I walked right smack into the middle of a construction site overrun with hard-hatted workers and their machinery. The noisy scene was unsettling to this pilgrim, arriving at long last at her destination.

Following signs pointing up a hill to "St. Julian's Church," I walked down St. Julian's Alley to the long-anticipated sight of the church with the anchorage. Both stay open to visitors and pilgrims all day, every day of the year, even during the 2020 pandemic. Many passersby on foot were heading elsewhere, much as they did in Julian's time.

A parish picnic the day before had kept me away one day longer than I planned. I did not wish to join a community at that auspicious moment in my pilgrimage. But when Monday came, I left early, hoping I would be the only one inside the church before the morning Mass. I wanted to be all alone with Julian.

Upon entering St. Julian's Church, I realized that would not be the case. A man was sitting alone in the sanctuary praying at the foot of a statue of Mary. When I peered through the double wooden doors into the anchorage for the first time, I saw a priest with a golden-retriever service dog and another man, sitting and talking side by side. This was an unwelcome sight to my pilgrim eyes. I selfishly wanted my welcome to come from Julian and no one else. As I turned to go out to the garden behind the church, I noticed a small table at the door with little pieces of paper and a pencil to write prayers. Without thinking, these words came to me: "For my heart to heal." It was the first time I wrote down what was to become my pilgrim prayer.

Once outside, I saw the exterior of Julian's anchorage for the first time. Its pitched-tile roof and large stained-glass window were familiar from photos I had seen on the internet. As I snapped photos, I heard the bell clang and clang.

> "The bell at St. Julian's church is engraved with the words 'AVE GRACIA PLENA DOMINUS TECUM' ('Hail full of grace, the Lord is with you'). It is called Gabriel, and still rings the Angelus to recall the angel's message to Mary. It dates from the 1400s, when people still alive would have known Julian."[1]

Entering the anchorage doors, I stepped down a few steps across the threshold, and said, "Good morning," while taking a seat on a long wooden bench along the inside wall. I looked up to see a huge wooden crucifix before me. Beneath it was an altar with a

1. Upjohn, *The Way of Julian.*

white cloth edged with embroidered golden anchors. Two white pillar candles were burning at either end.

A few women entered, hugged each other, petted the dog, and sat down. One of them took some small brass bells from the altar and placed them by her feet. Chitchat filled the room. When an older priest in his embroidered chasuble came into the anchorage, we all stood up in silence. He bowed silently before the altar and proceeded to celebrate Mass, moving through the words quickly without affect or emotion. At consecration of the bread and wine, the woman with the little bells reached down and jingled them, evoking in me memories of St. Marie's Church of my childhood. In that tiny church, the size of St. Julian's, I had made my First Communion. It is as "clear as a bell" sixty years hence.

Following the Mass, the women invited me to stay to pray the rosary with them. I felt honored. I told them I had intentionally left my own beads at home, not wanting to chance losing them in travel because they were a gift bought in Rome by my daughter. One of the women handed me her wooden beads.

"These are from Siena," she said softly, as we looked into each other's eyes. Her blond hair was tied in a bun. She wore very practical clothes. I was wearing one of my favorite skirts, which she said was "lovely." I held her wooden beads between my forefinger and thumb as we recited together the "Hail Mary" while she counted them out on her fingers.

It reminded me of mother's nightly ritual in our tiny living room. Each evening during the season of Lent, our whole family prayed the rosary. She made us kneel on the hardwood floor, as she did when she punished us. It was hard to tell the difference sometimes. Mother was relentless about this ritual, wanting all of us to be present. She insisted on Daddy's being in the room, too, despite having to wake him hours too early for his night shift. I hated it when she asked me to be the one to "go wake Daddy." He always obliged her and joined us on bended knees.

Each in our turn, we five children would say one of the five decades, and then Mother would recite the in-between beads.

My knees would be hurting when it was my turn to recite, so very quickly I said out loud, "Hail Mary, full of grace . . . Amen.

Hail Mary, full of grace . . . Amen." My heart was clearly not in the prayers in those days.

In the Norwich anchorage, women prayed together very thoughtfully and methodically. We took turns offering the call and response. It felt good to be included, as though two far-away worlds were intersecting through prayer.

One month to the day, back at home in my own anchorage in St. Augustine, I think about the six of us sitting like a family, praying the rosary together. As my fingers move over my own wooden beads in prayer, the San Sebastian River carries me away to an anchorage on another river that no longer seems so far away.

Foreclosing Options

Since my last day in Norwich, many things have become clear. The first "failed" attempt to make the pilgrimage a year earlier had left me wondering exactly why that happened. I accepted it by saying it had not been the "auspicious time," when all things move together. It had been suggested to me that, as in mythology, the door would not open until the right question was asked. And that another chance would come. It did. Months before the whole world was to close down in the face of a pandemic, I got on a plane as I had often done. There was no way for me to know then how significant that would seem in retrospect. Not only was travel about to be closed indefinitely, but the passing of a year between my first-planned flight and my actual pilgrimage brought Julian's plague experience together with my own pandemic experience.

The Julian story, as written by the anchoress, has survived the test of time. She has made a name for herself far beyond the confines of her small enclosure and small city walls. Her self-imposed exile was an interior pilgrimage she undertook in her anchoress cell.

"I love Julian" and "Julian is one of my favorites" are comments I often hear when I share my pilgrimage story. In some spiritual circles, Mother Julian, as she is affectionately called, is these days at the center of attention. How come?

When the coronavirus took hold of the world, Julian and her immortal words, *"All shall be well,"*[1] brought solace to many. I am glad that I made my pilgrimage when I had the chance.

1. Spearing, *Revelations of Divine Love*, 22.

I feel certain, to the relief of family and friends, that I will not become an anchoress, living as a solitary woman in St. Augustine. However, I have come to understand that I am not "a social butterfly," as my mother used to say of me. What then lies ahead?

The Forest Dweller Within

When I returned home to Florida, my sacred tree was standing its ground, as always. God willing, it will be there in 600 years, like Julian's anchorage. The sacred tree speaks to me about exile.

If a tree cannot know exile, it is in other ways like every other living, breathing thing, because it self-perpetuates. It does so, however, without moving an inch. A tree simply drops its seed from its arms onto the ground below. When a new tree grows from the smallest acorn, or the biggest pinecone, or tiniest hazelnut, it creates a new life, free of exile. Anchored in one place, and one place only, a tree remains forever connected to its source. Any longing to reconnect is therefore never part of its extensive life on earth, which is sometimes as much as a thousand years.

Julian writes of a tiny hazelnut she holds in her hand:

> *"I looked at it with my mind's eye and I thought, 'What can this be?' An answer came. It is all that is made. I marveled that it could last, for I thought it might have crumbled to nothing, it was so small. And, the answer came into my mind, `It lasts and ever shall because God loves it, and all things have being through the love of God.'"*[1]

The "anchoress" and the "forest dweller" have been doing battle in my psyche, masquerading as similar states of exile. I know they are not one and the same. Yet, each exists. Neither can be denied. I could not decide if I preferred one over the other, or why. Sometimes, I imagined myself living as an anchoress. Other times,

---

1. Spearing, *Revelations of Divine Love*, 47.

my "third life" seemed less about place and more about wandering, like a forest dweller.

The anchoress and the forest dweller both live in exile. Exile is about being separated from familiar people and places. It does not mean you are necessarily alone, but elsewhere, perhaps with different people. Separating is the first requirement of exile. Whether an anchoress, a forest dweller, or a mother, separating is required.

Most breathing beings experience a form of exile by separating from a mother at birth. To miraculously enter into existence is, by definition, a separation from one's source. That first separating breath is the beginning of one's own life in exile. And in that moment of separating, a yearning to be reconnected—not only to one's mother, but to the infinite source of all creation—begins to stir up a longing in heart and soul. This longing is a life force that has its origins in the act of separating. Separating is the essence of exile.

During many months of preparing for my pilgrimage, there were times when I could not understand Julian's choice to live in exile. In those moments, I felt that impulse of the forest dweller calling to me. The forest dweller can move about in a state of exile, while the anchoress must stay in a place of exile. The former, while separating from familiar people and places, makes some other world a dwelling while wandering in exile. The latter, the anchoress, likewise separating from familiar people and places, exists perpetually within her very particular place of exile.

I think I know the reason why I kept running into the forest dweller on my quest. When I was a young girl, I wandered about in the woods behind my home. Alone. I loved to climb my favorite tree, where I would sit and talk to God. I never felt the sense of "aloneness" that I certainly felt sitting alone in Julian's anchorage. Never. In that early experience of exile, that earliest separation from mother and family, the forest dweller in me was probably born.

I found a new world in the woods, an interior world in which to dwell. The birds were friends. The tree was more than that, it was a place where I felt at one with the One. Trees are a constant grounding and anchoring for me. I am at one with their life force and breath. I know and trust trees.

"One-ing" is Julian's word, but at the time I had no knowledge of the Anchoress of Norwich. She coined the word One-ing to speak about union with God. In her definition, there is no in-between one's soul and God. There is no borderland. She believed that the longing we inherit at birth is answered in that One-ing.

To live in exile, whether like Julian as an anchoress, or like the forest dweller in one's third life, may mean staying in exile for countless years. The choice to become an anchoress or a forest dweller requires a belief in a promising outcome. The promise itself calls. To answer that call, based on what may seem like a vague promise, requires trust and hope.

As a young girl, I was exiled from childhood. Life began simply and peacefully in my rural New England hometown. But that life was shattered within my first decade, leaving me bereft in the face of death, so many deaths, year after year. My childhood disappeared into what I call the "black ice." At times, things were as bad as in Julian's Dark Ages. Death was as familiar to me by age twelve, as if I, too, had lived through a plague. First, my own father, then my grandfather, followed by my grandmother on Christmas morning. In those years, I learned more about attending funerals than about living life. Yet, somehow, I sailed on, my anchor in tow.

Out of those early days of emptiness, I received something of grace: hope. It has been an anchor in my heart. Hope for what? Perhaps this is not exactly the right question. Hope is a transitive verb; it helps us move over the threshold into the future. Hope has done this for me many times after I have been standing still, abiding in place, before attempting a transition. In a sense, hope allowed me to see beyond, so I could move through, across, and over. With that also came a sense of knowing that I was always protected.

Some time ago, while traveling in Spain, my husband and I were riding bicycles through the piazza in Majorca. The bike was too big for me, and I couldn't maneuver through the crowd. When I swerved, the bike turned over, and I landed on the concrete sidewalk. I felt my head, without a helmet, hit that sidewalk on my right temple.

I heard Arthur's voice, "You're all right, sweetheart."

I felt the sunshine on my face as I lay sprawled on the ground. My eyes did not wish to open. I could sense people around.

I heard a man say, "Can you move your head?"

I opened my eyes. A dark-eyed Spaniard smiled. He was wearing white.

He said, "Does it hurt anywhere?"

I think I answered him.

"You are all right," he said, before he drifted away into the crowd that had gathered.

I got up slowly. Arthur and I moved the bikes and sat for a while on a park bench. There was a fountain with water rising and falling, forming the shape of a heart each time. I watched it glistening in the sunlight. It was mesmerizing. I thought about the man in white hovering over me. Was he an angel? Arthur brought me a gelato. I felt dazed. We walked slowly around the piazza. Looking downward as I stepped, I saw a sparrow lying on the curbside. It was not moving. I noticed on its temple a dried droplet of blood.

"Oh, it's dead," I said to myself.

The line of a hymn, "His eye is on the sparrow, and I know he watches me," popped into mind.

I wondered: "At the moment when my own right temple hit the sidewalk, did God take His eye off that sparrow to protect me?" I wonder still.

PART SIX

Return from Exile

Exile is a State of Mind

Cape Cod, Massachusetts

August 3, 2019

It took my daughter to teach me. She is wise, at times, beyond her years. It all came home to roost during a visit with her in our old house on Cape Cod. Memories I had long forgotten and thought I had let go, were rekindled and set ablaze. Hannah lit the match.

Her eyes looked puffy from crying.

Probing, in what I hoped was a gentle way, I asked:

"Are you all right?"

"I don't know why I feel so sad," she said softly.

Our shared story has been sometimes very sad. She had been too young at the time of the divorce to understand it all. I had my own sadness to process, leaving her to do the same in her own time. Adulthood had brought it back to her in the form of questions for which she wanted answers from me: "Why? Why did you? Why didn't you . . .? It wasn't fair."

She was holding back tears while speaking the unvarnished truth: It was not fair. We both broke down in tears.

Reliving our shared story reminded me of how and why I made decisions many years earlier to claim and to live in our Florida condo instead of staying in our Cape Cod home, where Hannah's dad now lives. I didn't try to explain to Hannah how that choice now feels like a self-imposed exile.

There was no crystal ball available to help me see ahead. As it turned out, my predictions about Hannah's own choices were only fifty-fifty. Had plans gone as I imagined, our ties to an old place would have broken when she went to college. During the intervening decade, both our lives changed. We changed. We are changing still.

For the better part of a year, I have been second-guessing my earlier decision to take the Florida condo rather than the house on Cape Cod. Was I wrong to think that Hannah would not choose to return to the Cape one day?

My own fate had been pre-determined at a mediation court.

"I want you to understand," said the black-robed judge, looking down from her high bench. "Some of these choices are permanent; you cannot come back to the court later," she said directly to me.

"Yes, your honor, I understand," I said, setting something in stone.

At the time, I thought going south would be one way to break ties with Hannah's dad. Cape Cod seemed too small for both of us. I knew I would have no real privacy in my effort to begin again until he made some fundamental changes.

"Why are you here?" I asked as he pulled the lawnmower from the backyard shed.

"I'm going to mow the lawn," he answered, as if he had never left; as if he still lived there.

That scene played out over and over in different ways during Hannah's waning high-school years. I was counting the days until she would go to college. I was eager to move out of the family homestead. A few weeks shy of her departure, I packed my belongings. She packed her own. We were going our separate ways. Sitting beside me, ten years later, in the living room where so much of her life had happened, she was telling me how painful that transition had been for her. It was like visiting a grave. I had no choice but to share the thoughts and feelings that led to my decisions:

"I thought I was protecting you by going quietly, so that you would not have to watch me leaving," I explained through big, wet tears streaming down my face. "I thought it would be easier if I . . . I didn't know how hard it would be on you." There was no way to change those decisions. All the emotional upheaval we had both endured was now visible in retrospect.

Each time I returned to visit her, we side-stepped unexploded emotional landmines. Until now. I might have avoided it once again, had Hannah not wandered into them. I did not want her to take that step alone. I followed gingerly, as all those old unspoken hurts were unearthed—*Ka-boom!* Right in my face.

Despite the pain of reliving this experience together, we hugged hard afterward. An evening walk at sunset, arm-in-arm on Breakwater Beach, created a new memory following the painful catharsis.

My own laments of late, about living in self-imposed exile in Florida, look different now. I see what was blinding me to the truth about my long-ago choice: Hannah's decision had put my own in question. My change of heart began when Hannah decided to live on the Cape.

We had never shared a good-bye there. We couldn't. I couldn't. These "strings attached" to each and every visit were the remaining unintended, unresolved consequences of our former life.

For My Heart to Heal

Cambridge, Massachusetts

September 9, 2019

I lifted my head just in time to see the familiar sycamore trees standing in a row in front of the monastery on Memorial Drive. A siren blared and the trees quickly receded from view as an ambulance rushed me to the hospital. I thought of the monks chanting evening prayer by candlelight. I wished I could join them this evening more than ever. Wiping a silent tear from my cheek, I prayed for angels to be with me.

A medic, seated beside me in the ambulance, was explaining my scribbled EKG:

"Most people can live with this sort of a-fib," he said. "Your heart is steadier now." Reaching above me to steady an I.V. swinging overhead, he added:

"They have better equipment at the Emergency Room."

Our arrival at Mt. Auburn Hospital was expected because nurses in the urgent care walk-in center at Harvard Square had called ahead. As they were calling, Hannah sent this text to me: "I just learned my friend's mother died. I love you." I could not take all of this in.

"I don't need to go by ambulance," I said to the nurses several times.

"Everyone says that. We'll make it worth your while with all the bells and whistles," one of them said insistently with a big smile. Finally, I agreed.

When the ambulance arrived at the hospital, the medic wheeled me through double doors while explaining my situation to a nurse in blue scrubs.

"She's a sixty-six-year-old woman who was seen at Harvard Services for heart palpitations, shortness of breath, and lightheadedness. Her EKG shows a slight a-fibrillation. She received an I.V. solution on the way."

He and another attendant lifted me in a blanket from a gurney to a bed in one swift motion. Without skipping a beat, each person in my tiny hospital room did a little dance around me. Arthur wound up in a chair in the corner, my bags and coat piled on his lap. His face said it all.

The evening progressed in slow motion. A big clock on the wall reminded me of one other time that I had been in a hospital. It appeared less as a timepiece and more as a preposterous decoration. I told Arthur that when I was in labor with Hannah, I had focused on another clock just like it.

"But I never noticed the time for the entire eight hours," I added. We smiled at one another in a brief moment of relief. Being in a hospital bed seemed incongruous with my entire life. The well-meaning doctors and nurses seemed reassuring on the one hand, but offered scenarios that did not resonate with my lifestyle.

"Your father died very young of a heart condition," the doctor said as he leaned over the side of the bedrail.

"I do not have the lifestyle he had at age forty-three," I replied. "He smoked unfiltered Lucky Strike cigarettes, had a meat-based diet, was overweight, and probably got little exercise."

"We only want to monitor you overnight," the doctor urged.

I felt like Alice in Wonderland, slipping through the looking glass. Who were all these strange characters in weird costumes? I heard myself exclaiming:

"This just does not fit with how I live my life. I eat well, exercise regularly, do not smoke, and I have a strong meditation and prayer practice. I have a strong faith."

My mind flashed back over the past three weeks of visiting family and friends in New England. I remembered that first day and the ferry crossing from Boston to Cape Cod.

"It looks like a great day to be on the water," I said to the attendant before boarding.

"Well," she replied, "it's actually pretty rough out there. We cancelled all the whale-watch boats. It's not too late to change your mind."

I decided to ride it out rather than rearrange my plans. I had been waiting six months to see my daughter. As the white caps bounced us around for ninety minutes, I focused my sight on that one steady point, the horizon line.

Eager to see family and friends, I had planned my itinerary according to each one's lifestyle. Come Sunday, I headed for church.

The Cape Cod Unitarian congregation was as alive as it had always been from the day of Hannah's christening to her high-school graduation. It felt right to be back there on a late summer morning. Yet, when we sang a familiar hymn:

> *"For the beauty of the earth, for the splendor of the sky,*
> *for the love which from our birth, over and around us lies,*
> *source of all to thee we raise, this our hymn of grateful*
> *praise,"*[1]

I started to cry.

It felt like the losses of a lifetime had come back to haunt me on the Cape, like a ghost of Christmas past. Walking away from the church without talking to anyone, I rented a bicycle and headed down a bike path, as I had often done to shake off sadness during my last years on Cape Cod. By this time, I was more than ready to get off the Cape and meet Arthur in Boston when he arrived as scheduled from Florida.

Our rendezvous was to have been at a favorite restaurant around the corner from our former apartment. I got there first. But when I walked into the hotel lobby and turned left, a gray wall greeted me rather than the colorful restaurant entrance.

"What happened to Brasserie Joe's?" I asked the concierge.

1. Pierpoint, *For the Beauty of the Earth.*

"It's closed for good," he said.

Arthur and I met for the first time in three weeks, out on the sidewalk.

Now we were sitting in an Emergency Room. My left ring finger was attached to a monitor, showing my very regular and steady heartbeat. An I.V. needle pushed fluid into my right arm. I kept thinking of my pilgrimage prayer: "For my heart to heal." I knew this prayer had followed me all the way from England to Cape Cod, then to Boston. Clearly, my heart needed to be healed. I remembered Julian's words: "*All shall be well.*"

One day after speeding past the monastery in an ambulance, I went there to pray as I had often done when I was a student nearby. Upon opening the heavy wooden door, the smell of incense soothed me. I had always been amazed that traffic noises were inaudible once that door closed behind me. Now, I wondered if sirens are, too. Without thinking, I sat exactly where I used to sit so long ago, when my life was spinning out of control. I remembered how desperately I had pleaded with God back then, barely able to control my tears. One of the monks recommended: "Ask for healing. Always ask for healing. Then look for it."

As I looked up at the very same crucifix hanging above the very same altar, a subtle smile came to my face and I mouthed the words: "Thank you." I could not express how grateful I felt to be alive and sitting there in the chapel. My heart felt like it was at last in a recovery room.

Heart Therapy

Peterborough, New Hampshire

September 15, 2019

At midnight, a full September moon lit up a mighty maple. I pulled a chair to the window. With my face turned upward like a sunflower toward the light, I watched the interplay of maple leaves and moonlight.

Distant sounds reverberated in the stillness. Sheep dogs barked out a warning. Owls sounded as loud as a train whistle, calling *Woo-woo.*

"I want to get home. I miss hearing the trains at night," I thought to myself. This visit with family in New Hampshire was my last stop before heading home.

I could hear Arthur's rhythmic breathing in the bed behind me. The rest of the house was still except for a dog's occasional shuffling on his window seat in the hallway. I looked down on the backyard below the maple, where earlier in the day we had laughed and played croquet in the afternoon sun. It was awash in white moonlight.

I stretched from my seat, looking for wickets we left in place for our next croquet game. Instead, I noticed an empty swing, hanging from two ropes on one of many sturdy limbs of the maple, said to be 350 years old. Its sprawling, leafy canopy had been an umbrella for our evening meal. A sun shower's gentle leaf-tapping went unheard by most of us, lost in conversation, the setting sun shining on our faces. Afterward, we were treated to a rainbow for dessert, a bright sherbet in the sky.

The middle of the night brings the world a bit closer. The stars seem reachable. The waning summer felt like a time capsule. Long weeks of travel had brought me back to old friends, old loves, old lives. I could not rationalize why so often I had lost love. I remembered lighting prayer candles on my pilgrimage and hearing those words: "For their hearts to heal."

Pilgrim's Prayer

I was in Julian's anchorage when I first asked "for my heart to heal." I tacked a small square of paper with my handwritten request onto a cork board on the wall. It stayed there while I wandered, as pilgrims do. On the final day of my pilgrimage, I noticed the prayer was still there.

Thrice these same words "For my heart to heal" were placed on altars to be read aloud sometime by someone within the sacred spaces of Ely and Norwich Cathedrals, as well as in Julian's anchorage. For some reason, whenever I recall writing those pilgrim prayers, I see myself wearing my old dark raincoat. Actually, I did not wear it at all on my trip to Norwich. I wonder if I am seeing that raincoat as a symbol of life's storms, from which I have sought protection for so long?

For many years, I prayed a different prayer. I had asked for my heart to remain "open without sharp edges or closed doors." I trusted that my prayer would keep me from being angry or becoming bitter. I would "watch and wait," and in that way I expected my prayers would be answered. I hoped against hope for lost love to return. At various times, this prayer appeared to me to be close to being answered. I held my breath whenever "missed" opportunities arose serendipitously. With each new disappointment, I interpreted the results as a sign of an answer yet to come. Nothing, as it turned out, was coming. That prayer did not bear fruit. That is the bitter truth.

Despite this, for years I could not let go. I believed if I stopped asking—stopped believing—I risked not receiving the answer to that prayer, the answer that I wanted. Letting go of that prayer was harder than waiting. In the end, an altogether different answer came through my pilgrim's prayer. The words "For my heart to heal" affected me more than I could have ever known when I first wrote that request in Julian's anchorage. Another very familiar prayer pushed me toward healing.

It was the one I have recited innumerable times since my own father was on earth. One day I heard a minister say: "The loneliest person in a foxhole is the one who does not know the 'Lord's Prayer.'" I made sure my daughter learned it immediately. The words of that prayer, recited by rote, had never grabbed me the way they did that day on my pilgrimage. Following twenty silent minutes of meditation, with my home-away-from-home meditation group at Norwich Cathedral, we recited together the "Lord's Prayer." When we came to the words *as we forgive those who trespass against us,* I saw my old love's face.

Soon afterward, I walked back into the busyness of the Cathedral grounds. The peregrines were screeching and soaring above the labyrinth. I sat down in the cloister.

"Have I ever forgiven him?" I asked myself.

Truth be told, I had never before that moment even considered it was something I needed to do. I had so unshakably believed that my prayer, "for my heart to have no sharp edges or closed doors," was what I needed. Closure was not what I had been asking for. My poor heart had been made to wait without healing for such a long, long time. Nobody but God knew I was a lady in waiting.

The waiting ended on my pilgrimage with this changed request: "for my heart to heal." And ultimately, through forgiveness, I made my peace with it all. God knows it was time.

Hazelnuts Heal Hearts

St. Augustine, Florida

October 1, 2019

The first week back in St. Augustine, I was thrown into cardio-medical tests that took me out of my comfort zone. I could have lived without it, but maybe not. Who is to say? That question loomed as a plethora of medical marvels were offered to a mere mortal like me. This turn of events, in my heretofore healthy life, is part of a timely ironic twist. My prayer that began in Julian's anchorage, "For my heart to heal," has had far-reaching effects beyond my wildest expectations. Be careful what you pray for.

Also, Julian's hazelnut has taken on new meaning. I kept one for myself, taken from the anchorage as a touchstone of my pilgrimage. It traveled with me from Julian's altar to mine along with a candlestick I bought at the Julian Center. When I light that candle, I recall vividly sitting in her anchorage.

Since my recent experience in the Emergency Room, I have been performing my "due diligence" regarding heart and health. Just the other day, I sat at my computer researching "heart healthy food." Hazelnuts popped up:

"Hazelnuts provide a cholesterol-free energy source. They're packed with healthy fats, including omega-3s, which can be good for your heart."[1]

The first time I read this, the connection with Julian escaped me, focused was I on rushing to medical answers that might help me fend off heart disease in the future.

"Oh, good. I love hazelnuts." I thought. Within a few days, as though a lightning bolt struck me, I said out loud:

"Hazelnuts heal hearts!"

My prayer "for my heart to heal," placed on Julian's very own altar, along with those hazelnuts, was being answered not only spiritually, but literally. How could I have known that within a month of my pilgrimage, I would be eating hazelnuts by the handful?

Hazelnuts contain a secret I need in more ways than one. They have become, in a true sense, the boon, the gift of my pilgrimage. I had felt my heart healing emotionally, but now I needed a physical healing, too. Hazelnuts meant nothing to me before I went on my pilgrimage. Nothing. Ironically, I wanted to find one while in Norwich, thinking this might be a tangible link between our shared stories of self-imposed exile. To my surprise, I found a basketful of hazelnuts inside the door to Julian's anchorage. They looked like acorns that I had raked up each fall in my childhood backyard. I took a handful from the basket and placed some on the altar while thinking of my friends and family back home.

I kept just one for myself in my backpack. My pilgrim shell was attached as my only outward sign that I was a pilgrim on a pilgrimage. Scallop shells have been a symbol of pilgrimage since early pilgrims wandered the countryside to do penance. When I was served tea at the Julian Center, a hazelnut was cut in two in the saucer. I saw then for the first time the inside of the nut.

Julian's words aptly describe her life as Anchoress of St. Julian's Church, living within a self-contained anchorage—like a hazelnut shell that contains the whole cosmos:

"He shewed me a little thing, the quantity of an hazel-nut, in the palm of my hand; and it was as round as a ball. I looked thereupon

---

1. www.WebMD.com

with eye of my understanding, and thought: What may this be? And it was answered generally thus: it is all that is made. I marvelled how it might last, for methought it might suddenly have fallen to naught for little[ness]. And I was answered in my understanding: It lasteth, and ever shall [last] for that God loveth it. And so All-thing hath the Being by the love of God."

The pilgrimage to the anchorage had called me. There was something waiting for me there in Norwich, I just knew it. I did not know what, but I was compelled to go. Being thwarted in my first attempt, I was made to wait for the auspicious time to go, God's time. A year hence, all the pieces fell into place perfectly. The journey is now complete. The healing goes on. The understanding grows.

Revelations of an Exile

The pilgrimage had carried me over the threshold and out of self-imposed exile. I had heard a voice to go. I had followed. That voice was familiar. I had heard it other times. This time, the voice came as I stepped into the bath:

"This pain is not physical." I heard it clearly.

As I sat watching the flickering of candlelight reflected in the bath water, I thought about the heartaches that had plagued me since summer.

"Aaah! This pain is not physical," I said out loud. I understood there and then that my heart was suffering from emotional and psychological pain.

Loss had found me everywhere this past summer. My heart had broken again and again under the weight of "the hopes and fears of all the years."[1] It had hurt like the first time—only more.

That familiar "voice" comes when I am alone. Or, should I say, by myself, as I am never truly alone. Today, I spoke back to the unseen voice because I wanted to know: "How was this sense of one-ness, this hope in things unseen, imparted to me when I was young and my life was bleak and without a foreseeable future? How? And how is it I did not impart this same sense of hope to my own daughter?"

Her childhood did not resemble mine, but like me she suffered losses. She, like me, had cherished the family ideal. She, like me, had to face the fact of life's losses early. Yet, our views clash; our beliefs differ; our hope in things unseen is like night and day.

1. Brooks, *O Little Town of Bethlehem*

Do we need to see what the other sees to really understand one another? Does it matter? Our conversations, riddled with past hurts, do not well serve either of us any longer. That is the truth.

We know Truth when we see it or hear it. It speaks loudly from within giving all the answers to all the questions, if only we listen. Such revelations open the way to our own soulful truth. Moments of revelation in my lifetime have appeared then disappeared: that day in the bookstore; the time reading the newspaper; the airport tornado closure; now, the voice I "heard" in the bath. Each revelation remains even while dissipating like a dream, where there is no horizon line dividing there from here.

After thirty years—half of my adult life and the full lifetime of my daughter—I went seeking at long last to heal an old unhealed wound. I got more than I had hoped for from my pilgrim prayer: That prayer helped us to peel off old mother/daughter scabs, together. We faced the pain we had carried individually; something so difficult we could not speak of it until we were both ready. As we walked together hand-in-hand into our past, I had felt the physical pain in my heart.

In the months since returning home to Florida I suffered actual, physical heart pain. I focused on finding an answer through medical means. I did not fully understand that this was true heartache, born of compounded losses that I no longer needed to bear or to deny. The answer to my prayer, "For my heart to heal," came in that voice telling me: "This pain is not physical."

That unspeakable "silent voice" is as mysterious as a mystic's vision. To hear it is to know. The more you know, the less you have to say.

Epilogue

Outside my window, the leaves of the crepe myrtle have turned fiery red. Fall has turned to winter, marking the end of this prolonged pandemic year. During this time, much has been revealed to me while in exile. Many events happened serendipitously rather than by design, i.e., my design. Now that the whole web of the story can be seen, the embroidered threads underneath show a knotted mess.

"Life is messy," said a wise man I met along the way.

I had not anticipated dwelling in the borderlands of long-past episodes of my life. Trying to make sense of it all requires stopping the clock on ordinary time. That is exactly what exile does. Exile stops everything. All that went before begins to slip away. What remains is "once upon a time," in the way that a photograph captures something long ago, but not forgotten: "Look, remember what it was like there and then, when your hair was dark?"

Photographs press the stop button on time, twice. First, in that moment of inception. Then again when that same photo reappears as an old photo with a story to tell, like my graduation photograph, absent me.

My brother has our parents' wedding photograph on the wall in his living room. Presumably taken on their wedding day, it shows a full-front view in black and white of a young man in uniform, hat in hand, standing beside a soon-to-be thirty-year-old woman in a long white gown, holding a bouquet of flowers. They look out at me, a testament to their future, without regard for me staring back at them. All the while, they smile quietly. I, from my unique vantage point, like standing atop the Matterhorn, could tell them what lies beyond their horizon line at the *"blue zenith, the point where romance and reality meet,"*[1] as Emerson puts it.

If I could, I would ask them what their dreams and hopes were in that moment of their life together. I would ask my mother if my father was the love of her life.

Photos tell true stories captured in a fraction of a second in the middle of what was and what is yet to be. The truth cannot be denied. Yet, more than that, photographs take a measure of life while it is being lived. Nobody could see or say or know the couple's whole life story on that day. The in-between time cannot be seen like the vanishing point where all becomes one.

Seven decades later, their true story speaks to me, their daughter. Seven centuries ago, Julian of Norwich spoke her true story. It continues to speak across the ages to her "even-Christians," most especially during another time of plague.

After a long reckoning, an exile, and a pilgrimage, I can honestly say that some parts of my story have at last been exposed, like a photo capturing some moment of truth.

1. Emerson, *Nature.*

Bibliography

Boeckmann, Catherine, "Watch For January's Full Wolf Moon!"
The Old Farmer's Almanac, 2020. https://www.almanac.com/content/.

Brooks, Phillips, "O little town of Bethlehem," 1868.

Cambridge Dictionary, https://dictionary.cambridge.org/us/, 2021.

Cousineau, Phil. *The Art of Pilgrimage The Seeker's Guide to Making Travel Sacred.* Berkeley, CA: Conari, 1998.

Cressy, R.F.S. *Juliana, Mother, Anchorite of Norwich: XVI Revelations of Divine Love.* Sloane Manuscript 2499, 1670. The British Library London, England.

Emerson, Ralph W. "Nature." The Project Gutenberg EBook of Essays, Second Series, by Ralph Waldo Emerson, 2009. https://www.gutenberg.org/.

Gibran, Kahlil, *The Prophet.* New York, New York: Alfred A. Knopf, 1940. https://www.goodreads.com/.

Julian of Norwich Revelations of Divine Love. Translated by Elizabeth and A.C. Spearing. London, England: Penguin, 1998.

Leo Tolstoy A Confession and Other Religious Writings. Translated by Jane Kentish. London, England: Penguin, 1987.

Nourish by WebMD. "Health benefits of hazelnuts." https://www.webmd.com/. n.d.

Pierpoint, Folliott S., and Conrad Kocher. "For the Beauty of the Earth." https://www.uua.org/. n.d.

Upjohn, Sheilah, *The Way of Julian of Norwich A Prayer Journey Through Lent.* London, England: SPCK, Kindle, 2020.

Ward, Benedicta, "The Desert of the Heart: Daily Readings with the Desert Fathers." London, England: Darton, Longman and Todd, 1998. https://citydesert.wordpress.com/.